"Elias Thorne delivers a crucial guide to understanding AI's transformative potential in mental healthcare. It offers accessible insights and addresses ethical concerns. A must-read for anyone shaping the future of wellbeing."

THE FUTURE OF

AI

— IN —

MENTAL HEALTHCARE

A Guide to Understanding Generative AI, Transforming Mental Healthcare, and Improving Lives

ELIAS THORNE

First published by Purple Fox Publications 2025

First Edition

Paperback
ISBN: 9798315227236

Hardback
ISBN: 9798315227496

Contents

The Mental Health Landscape: Needs, Gaps, and Opportunities

The Current State of Mental Health: A Global Perspective

The story of mental health in the 21st century is one of both progress and profound challenge. While awareness and understanding have increased significantly in recent years, the global burden of mental illness remains staggering. To understand the potential of AI in this field, we must first confront the realities of the present landscape.

Overview of Common Mental Health Conditions: Prevalence, Impact, and Associated Costs

A crucial first step is to assess common mental health conditions across the globe, examining their prevalence, the far-reaching impacts they have on society, and the considerable economic costs associated with them. These are not isolated concerns; they represent a complex web of interconnected issues impacting communities and economies worldwide. Globally, mental health conditions affect hundreds of millions of people. Depression,

7

anxiety disorders, bipolar disorder, schizophrenia, and eating disorders are among the most common, each presenting unique challenges for individuals and healthcare systems.

The prevalence rates vary across different regions and populations due to a complex interplay of factors, including socioeconomic conditions, cultural norms, and access to resources. For example, studies indicate that depression is more prevalent in low-income countries, where individuals often face greater adversity and limited access to mental healthcare. These high rates of mental health conditions have profound impacts on individuals, families, and communities. Mental illness can lead to decreased productivity, absenteeism from work or school, strained relationships, and increased risk of substance abuse and suicide. Furthermore, the stigma associated with mental illness often prevents individuals from seeking help, perpetuating a cycle of suffering and isolation.

The economic costs of mental illness are equally significant. According to the World Health Organization, mental health conditions represent a substantial economic burden globally, costing trillions of dollars each year. These costs are not only direct, such as the expense of treatment and medication, but also indirect, including lost productivity, disability benefits, and premature mortality. Investing in mental healthcare, therefore, is not just a matter of compassion but also an economic imperative. It is clear that the existing mental health infrastructure is struggling to meet the growing demands of the global population. Understanding these conditions, their prevalence, and their costs will allow us to explore how AI can be employed to help solve these issues.

Challenges in Access to Care: Geographical Limitations, Affordability Barriers, and Stigma

While the global understanding of mental health issues has increased, significant challenges remain in ensuring equitable access to care. These challenges are multifaceted, ranging from geographical limitations and affordability barriers to the persistent stigma surrounding mental illness. Overcoming these obstacles is critical to bridging the gap between the growing need for mental healthcare and the resources available. Geographic limitations create immense obstacles for individu-

8

als living in rural or remote areas. Access to mental health professionals is often limited or non-existent in these regions, forcing individuals to travel long distances to seek treatment, an option that simply isn't viable for many. Telehealth solutions are emerging as a promising avenue, yet infrastructure limitations, such as lack of reliable internet connectivity, can hinder their effectiveness in these areas.

Affordability acts as another major roadblock, particularly in countries without universal healthcare systems. Even in nations with public healthcare, mental health services often receive inadequate funding, leading to long waiting lists and limited availability of specialized treatments. The cost of therapy, medication, and hospitalization can be prohibitive for individuals and families, forcing many to forgo necessary care. The economic burden is even greater for those from marginalized communities, who already face systemic disadvantages and financial instability.

Perhaps the most pervasive and insidious barrier is the stigma surrounding mental illness. Deep-seated societal beliefs and misconceptions can lead to discrimination, shame, and silence, preventing individuals from seeking help. This stigma can manifest in various forms, from negative stereotypes and prejudice to social exclusion and internalized shame. Addressing this complex issue requires a multifaceted approach that includes public awareness campaigns, education initiatives, and efforts to promote empathy and understanding. It's clear that addressing these geographical, economic and societal hurdles will be vital to increasing the number of people getting the help they need.

The Impact of Recent Global Events (e.g., Pandemic) on Mental Health Needs

The already strained global mental health landscape has been further exacerbated by recent global events, most notably the COVID-19 pandemic. The pandemic served as a magnifying glass, exposing and intensifying pre-existing vulnerabilities and creating new challenges for individuals across the globe. Understanding the specific ways in which these events have impacted mental health needs is essential for developing effective and targeted interventions. The widespread lockdowns, social isolation, economic uncertainty, and fear of infection took a significant toll on mental wellbeing. Studies have revealed a surge in anxiety, depression, and stress-related disorders during the pandemic, affecting individuals of all ages and backgrounds. Frontline healthcare workers, in particular, experienced immense psychological strain due to the high levels of stress, trauma, and burnout they faced.

Beyond the immediate impact of the pandemic, the long-term consequences on mental health remain a concern. The loss of loved ones, financial hardship, and disruption to routines have created a ripple effect that will likely continue to impact individuals and communities for years to come. Furthermore, the pandemic has disproportionately affected vulnerable populations, such as those with pre-existing mental health conditions, individuals from marginalized communities, and children and adolescents. The pandemic has also highlighted the interconnectedness of physical and mental health. The stress and anxiety associated with the pandemic can weaken the immune system, making individuals more susceptible to illness. Conversely, physical health conditions can increase the risk of mental health problems.

Addressing these challenges requires a comprehensive and integrated approach that considers the unique needs of different populations. Investing in mental health services, promoting mental health literacy, and addressing the social determinants of health are essential steps to mitigate the long-term impact of global events on mental wellbeing. The events of the last few years have changed society, and mental health needs must adapt to accommodate that.

Traditional Approaches and Their Limitations
Review of Traditional Therapy Models (e.g., CBT, Psychodynamic Therapy)

For decades, traditional therapy models have formed the bedrock of mental healthcare, providing individuals with valuable tools and techniques for managing their mental wellbeing. Understanding the core principles of these models is essential to appreciating the potential role of AI in enhancing and extending their reach. Cognitive Behavioral Therapy (CBT) stands as one of the most widely practiced and empirically supported approaches. CBT focuses on identifying and modifying negative thought patterns and behaviors that contribute to mental health problems. Therapists work with individuals to challenge these maladaptive thoughts and develop healthier coping mechanisms.

10

CBT has proven effective for a range of conditions, including anxiety disorders, depression, and obsessive-compulsive disorder.

Psychodynamic therapy, rooted in the work of Sigmund Freud, emphasizes the exploration of unconscious processes and past experiences to understand current behavior patterns. This approach often involves delving into early childhood relationships and unresolved conflicts to gain insight into present-day challenges. Psychodynamic therapy can be a longer-term process, aiming for deep personal transformation and improved self-awareness. Other therapeutic approaches, such as interpersonal therapy (IPT), focus on improving communication and relationship skills to address mental health issues. IPT recognizes the importance of social connections and the impact of interpersonal relationships on mental wellbeing. Mindfulness-based therapies, such as mindfulness-based stress reduction (MBSR), incorporate mindfulness practices, such as meditation and body scan techniques, to cultivate present moment awareness and reduce stress. These traditional models have proven effective in helping millions of people.

Limitations of Traditional Approaches: Therapist Availability, Cost, Waiting Lists, and Potential for Human Bias

Despite the established efficacy of traditional therapy models, significant limitations hinder their widespread accessibility and effectiveness. These limitations include challenges related to therapist availability, the high cost of treatment, lengthy waiting lists, and the potential for human bias to influence therapeutic outcomes. Addressing these shortcomings is crucial for creating a more equitable and accessible mental healthcare system. One of the most significant hurdles is the limited availability of qualified therapists, particularly in rural or underserved areas. The demand for mental health services often outstrips the supply of providers, leaving many individuals without access to timely and appropriate care. This shortage is further compounded by the uneven distribution of therapists across different geographic regions and socio-economic groups.

The cost of traditional therapy can also be a major barrier for many individuals, particularly those without adequate health insurance coverage. The hourly rates for therapy sessions can be prohibitive, making it difficult for individuals with limited financial resources to afford ongoing treatment. Even with insurance, copays and deductibles can add up, creating a financial burden for individuals and families. Lengthy waiting lists for therapy appointments are another common challenge, particularly in publicly funded mental health systems. Individuals may have to wait weeks or even months to see a therapist, delaying access to much-needed care. These delays can be particularly detrimental for individuals experiencing acute mental health crises, as prompt intervention is essential to prevent further deterioration.

The potential for human bias to influence therapeutic outcomes is a subtle but important consideration. Therapists, like all individuals, can be subject to unconscious biases that may affect their perceptions, interpretations, and treatment recommendations. These biases can stem from various factors, including cultural background, personal experiences, and societal stereotypes. While ethical guidelines and professional training aim to minimize bias, it is not always possible to eliminate it entirely. These limitations are preventing millions of people from getting the mental health support they need.

The Role of Medication in Mental Health Treatment: Benefits, Side Effects, and Limitations

Alongside therapy, medication plays a significant role in the treatment of many mental health conditions, offering relief from symptoms and improving overall functioning. Understanding the benefits, side effects, and limitations of medication is essential for making informed decisions about treatment options. Medications can be effective in managing a wide range of mental health conditions, including depression, anxiety disorders, bipolar disorder, schizophrenia, and ADHD. Antidepressants, for example, can help to regulate mood and reduce symptoms of depression by affecting the levels of neurotransmitters in the brain. Anti-anxiety medications can help to calm the nervous system and reduce feelings of anxiety and panic.

While medications can be beneficial, they are not without potential side effects. Common side effects of antidepressants can include weight gain, sexual dysfunction, and sleep disturbances. Anti-anxiety medications can cause drowsiness, dizziness, and cognitive impairment.

Some medications can also have more serious side effects, such as liver damage or heart problems. It is important for individuals to discuss the potential risks and benefits of medication with their healthcare provider before starting treatment.

The effectiveness of medication can vary from person to person, and not everyone responds well to medication. Some individuals may experience significant symptom relief, while others may not see any improvement. In some cases, individuals may need to try several different medications before finding one that works for them. Additionally, medication is often most effective when combined with other forms of treatment, such as therapy. Medication can help to stabilize symptoms and make it easier for individuals to engage in therapy, while therapy can help individuals develop coping skills and address underlying issues. It is essential to also take into consideration the cultural or personal beliefs surrounding mental health treatment, as well as the stigma that can be associated with needing or taking medication.

Introducing the Potential of AI: A Glimmer of Hope
Briefly Introduce the Concept of Artificial Intelligence (AI) and Its Different Forms

Against the backdrop of these challenges and limitations within traditional mental healthcare, a glimmer of hope emerges in the form of Artificial Intelligence (AI). AI represents a paradigm shift in how we approach problem-solving, offering innovative solutions to address long-standing issues across various sectors, including healthcare. Understanding the fundamental concepts of AI and its diverse forms is essential to appreciating its potential role in transforming mental healthcare. At its core, AI refers to the ability of machines to simulate human intelligence processes, such as learning, reasoning, problem-solving, and decision-making. This is achieved through complex algorithms and statistical models that enable computers to analyze vast amounts of data, identify patterns, and make predictions.

AI is not a monolithic entity but rather encompasses a range of different approaches and techniques. Machine learning (ML) is a subset of AI that focuses on enabling computers to learn from data without explicit programming. In ML, algorithms are trained on large datasets to identify patterns and make predictions about new data. Deep learn-

13

ing (DL) is a more advanced form of ML that utilizes artificial neural networks with multiple layers to analyze complex data, such as images, text, and audio. These deep learning algorithms can automatically extract features from raw data, eliminating the need for manual feature engineering.

Another important area of AI is natural language processing (NLP), which focuses on enabling computers to understand and process human language. NLP techniques are used in a variety of applications, such as chatbots, machine translation, and sentiment analysis. Expert systems are AI systems that use rule-based reasoning to solve problems in a specific domain. These systems typically rely on knowledge acquired from human experts to make decisions. AI is developing and improving at an increasingly rapid rate, and can provide a potential solution to many mental health care issues.

Highlight the Potential of AI in Addressing Gaps in Mental Healthcare Access and Affordability

The limitations within traditional mental healthcare, specifically those related to access and affordability, provide fertile ground for AI-driven solutions. AI has the potential to dramatically expand access to mental health services, particularly for underserved populations in remote areas or with limited financial resources. By automating certain tasks and providing remote support, AI can help to overcome geographical barriers and reduce the cost of treatment. AI-powered chatbots and virtual assistants can provide accessible and affordable mental health support, offering individuals convenient and on-demand access to evidence-based interventions. These tools can deliver personalized support, emotional validation, and coping strategies, supplementing or even replacing traditional therapy in some cases. The 24/7 availability of these resources allows individuals to receive support whenever and wherever they need it, overcoming the limitations of traditional office hours.

AI can also play a crucial role in reducing the cost of mental healthcare. By automating administrative tasks, such as appointment scheduling and billing, AI can free up mental health professionals to focus on providing direct patient care. AI-driven diagnostic tools can also

14

help to improve efficiency by identifying individuals at risk for mental health conditions and prioritizing them for treatment. Furthermore, AI can facilitate the development of personalized treatment plans, matching individuals with the most effective interventions based on their specific needs and preferences. This precision approach can help to avoid costly trial-and-error processes and optimize treatment outcomes.

AI can also overcome the financial barriers for treatment. This is especially important in regions with limited resources, where costs can prevent many people from getting the help they need. While traditional therapy may be beyond reach, AI offers alternative methods for people to find support and treatment options. This approach not only addresses immediate needs but also lays the groundwork for a healthcare system that is more equitable and responsive to the needs of all individuals.

Outline the Book's Roadmap for Exploring the Future of AI in Mental Health

This book embarks on a comprehensive journey to explore the transformative potential of AI in reshaping the landscape of mental healthcare. From demystifying the underlying technologies to examining real-world applications and addressing ethical considerations, this roadmap will equip readers with the knowledge and insights necessary to navigate this rapidly evolving field. The journey begins by providing a foundational understanding of generative AI, exploring its core concepts, training processes, and historical evolution. We will delve into the ethical considerations surrounding AI in mental health, examining issues such as privacy, bias, and transparency to ensure responsible implementation.

The book will then explore a variety of specific AI applications in mental healthcare, focusing on AI-powered chatbots, diagnostic tools, and content creation for mental wellbeing. Each application will be examined through the lens of real-world examples, case studies, and potential limitations. We will then confront the challenges associated with AI adoption, addressing regulatory hurdles, building trust and acceptance, and ensuring adequate infrastructure and investment. We will emphasize the crucial role of the human-AI partnership, exploring how mental health professionals can collaborate with AI to enhance their practice and improve patient outcomes.

In the later stages of the book, we will look to the future, examining emerging trends and innovations such as virtual reality therapy in the metaverse and AI-powered wearables for real-time mental health monitoring. We will focus on the role of AI in prevention, exploring how technology can be used to promote mental wellbeing and resilience. In closing, this book seeks to provide a balanced perspective, acknowledging both the immense potential of AI and the importance of responsible innovation. It is an invitation to embrace the future with optimism, caution, and a commitment to building a more equitable and accessible mental healthcare system for all.

Demystifying Generative AI: What It Is and How It Works

Defining Generative AI: Concepts and Key Technologies

What is generative AI? A clear and accessible explanation.

Generative AI, at its most fundamental level, refers to a class of artificial intelligence algorithms capable of producing new content, be it text, images, audio, or even code. Unlike traditional AI, which is typically designed to analyze or classify existing data, generative AI models are trained to learn the underlying patterns and structures within a dataset and then use this knowledge to create novel, original content that resembles the training data. Think of it as an AI that doesn't just understand a style, but can produce works within that style.

This capability stems from advanced machine learning techniques, particularly deep learning, which allows these models to learn complex representations of data. The implications of this technology are far-reaching, extending beyond simple replication to true creation. Generative AI is not just about copying what exists but about exploring new possibilities and pushing the boundaries of what's possible.

This holds significant promise in mental healthcare, where personalized and engaging content can be critical for improving patient outcomes and promoting wellbeing. For example, generative AI can be used to create personalized meditation scripts, generate unique art therapy prompts, or even develop realistic virtual environments for exposure therapy. The key lies in understanding the underlying technologies that power this transformative capability.

Overview of different generative AI models: Large Language Models (LLMs), image generators, etc.

Within the realm of generative AI, a diverse ecosystem of models has emerged, each specializing in generating different types of content. Among the most prominent are Large Language Models (LLMs), image generators, and audio synthesis models. Each of these model types leverages unique architectural designs and training techniques to achieve its specific generative capabilities.

Large Language Models (LLMs), such as GPT-3 and LaMDA, have revolutionized the field of natural language processing. These models are trained on massive datasets of text and code, enabling them to generate human-quality text, translate languages, write different kinds of creative content, and answer your questions in an informative way. Their ability to understand and generate nuanced language makes them particularly promising for mental health applications, such as creating personalized chatbot responses, generating therapeutic content, and facilitating natural language interactions in virtual therapy sessions.

Image generators, like DALL-E 2 and Stable Diffusion, have demonstrated the astonishing ability to create realistic and imaginative images from textual descriptions. These models utilize deep learning techniques, such as generative adversarial networks (GANs) and diffusion models, to learn the complex relationships between text and images. Image generators offer creative avenues for mental health interventions, such as creating personalized visualizations for guided imagery, generating art therapy prompts, or developing virtual environments for

18

exposure therapy. Audio synthesis models, including those used for text-to-speech and music generation, offer unique opportunities to create calming and therapeutic audio experiences. These models can generate realistic speech, personalized soundscapes, and even original music compositions tailored to individual preferences.

Understanding the capabilities and limitations of each generative AI model is essential for identifying the most appropriate tools for specific mental health applications. The technology is constantly evolving, and new models are appearing, each with its own strengths.

Basic concepts: neural networks, machine learning, deep learning.

To truly grasp the power of generative AI, it is necessary to understand the fundamental concepts that underpin its functionality: neural networks, machine learning, and deep learning. These three concepts are interconnected, with each building upon the previous one to create increasingly sophisticated AI systems.

Machine learning (ML) provides the foundation for generative AI. ML is a branch of artificial intelligence that focuses on enabling computers to learn from data without being explicitly programmed. Instead of relying on pre-defined rules, machine learning algorithms learn patterns and relationships from data, allowing them to make predictions or decisions about new data.

Neural networks are a specific type of machine learning algorithm inspired by the structure and function of the human brain. They consist of interconnected nodes, or neurons, organized in layers. Each connection between neurons has a weight associated with it, which represents the strength of the connection. Neural networks learn by adjusting these weights based on the input data they receive.

Deep learning (DL) takes neural networks to the next level by using networks with many layers (hence the term "deep"). These deep neural networks can learn more complex patterns and representations from data than traditional neural networks. Deep learning has been instrumental in the recent advances in generative AI, enabling models to generate highly realistic and creative content.

19

Understanding these basic concepts is crucial for anyone seeking to explore the potential of generative AI in mental healthcare. While the mathematical details of these algorithms can be complex, the core principles are relatively straightforward. This knowledge empowers individuals to critically evaluate AI solutions and identify opportunities for innovation in the field.

How Generative AI is Trained: Data, Algorithms, and Learning Processes
The role of data in training generative AI models.

The remarkable capabilities of generative AI are not achieved through magic but through a rigorous training process that relies heavily on vast amounts of data. Data serves as the fuel that powers the learning process, enabling these models to identify patterns, learn relationships, and generate new content that reflects the characteristics of the training data. The quality, quantity, and diversity of the training data have a profound impact on the performance and creativity of generative AI models. To generate realistic and diverse content, generative AI models require massive datasets that capture the full range of variations and nuances within the target domain. For example, a generative AI model designed to create personalized meditation scripts would need to be trained on a large collection of existing meditation scripts, encompassing different styles, themes, and target audiences.

The data must also be of high quality. If the training data contains errors, biases, or inconsistencies, the generative AI model will likely learn these flaws and reproduce them in the generated content. Therefore, careful data curation and cleaning are essential steps in the training process. Diversity is also a key consideration. If the training data is limited or biased, the generative AI model may struggle to generalize to new situations or create content that reflects the diversity of the real world. For example, a generative AI model trained solely on text written by men may exhibit gender bias in its language and content. The source data is an incredibly important element to creating good AI.

Explanation of the training process: supervised learning, unsupervised learning, and reinforcement learning.

The process of training generative AI models involves a va-

20

riety of learning paradigms, each with its unique approach to extracting knowledge from data. Supervised learning, unsupervised learning, and reinforcement learning represent three distinct but complementary methods for training these sophisticated systems. Supervised learning involves training a model on a labeled dataset, where each data point is paired with a corresponding output or target variable.

The model learns to map the input data to the output variable, allowing it to make predictions about new, unseen data. For example, in mental healthcare, supervised learning could be used to train a model to predict the likelihood of a patient developing depression based on their medical history and demographic information.

Unsupervised learning, on the other hand, involves training a model on an unlabeled dataset, where the model must discover patterns and relationships in the data without explicit guidance. This approach can be used to identify clusters of patients with similar characteristics, detect anomalies in mental health data, or learn representations of mental health concepts from unstructured text data.

Reinforcement learning involves training a model to make decisions in an environment to maximize a reward signal. The model learns through trial and error, receiving feedback in the form of rewards or penalties for its actions. In mental healthcare, reinforcement learning could be used to train a virtual therapist to provide personalized interventions to patients, adjusting its approach based on the patient's responses. These three learning styles combine to help AI analyze data.

Examples of publicly available generative AI and how it's being used.

The theoretical concepts behind generative AI come to life when examining the numerous publicly available tools and platforms leveraging this technology. These accessible resources provide a glimpse into the diverse applications of generative AI and its potential impact across various domains. Exploring these examples can provide valuable insights into how generative AI can be harnessed for mental healthcare.

One of the most well-known examples is GPT-3 (Generative Pre-trained Transformer 3), a large language model developed by OpenAI. GPT-3 can generate human-quality text for a wide range of tasks, including writing articles, composing emails, and answering questions. It is being used in applications like creating chatbots that provide personalized mental health support and generating educational content about mental wellbeing.

DALL-E 2, another creation of OpenAI, is an image generator that can create realistic and imaginative images from textual descriptions. DALL-E 2 allows users to generate art therapy prompts, creating personalized visualizations for guided imagery, or designing virtual environments for exposure therapy.

Other examples include platforms that allow users to create personalized music playlists based on their mood and preferences. These platforms use AI algorithms to analyze the acoustic characteristics of music and generate playlists that are tailored to evoke specific emotional responses. These are merely a few of the examples that are available to the public.

The Evolution of Generative AI: A Historical Perspective
Tracing the historical development of AI from early conceptualizations to modern generative models.

The remarkable capabilities of today's generative AI models are the result of decades of research and development, building upon early conceptualizations of artificial intelligence. Tracing the historical development of AI provides valuable context for understanding the current state of the field and anticipating future trends.

The origins of AI can be traced back to the mid-20th century, with the development of early computer programs capable of solving logical problems and playing games. These early AI systems relied on rule-based reasoning and symbolic manipulation, rather than the data-driven learning approaches that characterize modern AI.

The field of neural networks emerged in the 1950s, inspired by the structure and function of the human brain. However, early neural network models were limited by their computational capabilities and lack of training data. Machine learning algorithms, such as decision

22

trees and support vector machines, gained prominence in the late 20th century, offering more efficient and scalable approaches to learning from data. The advent of deep learning in the 21st century marked a major breakthrough in AI, enabling neural networks with multiple layers to learn complex patterns and representations from data. This deep learning revolution, coupled with the availability of massive datasets and increased computing power, paved the way for the development of modern generative AI models. This long history has helped give rise to where generative AI is today.

Key milestones in the evolution of generative AI: breakthroughs in algorithms, hardware, and data availability.

Several key milestones have punctuated the evolution of generative AI, each representing a significant leap forward in capabilities and potential. These milestones are a combination of algorithmic breakthroughs, advancements in hardware, and the growing availability of data. The development of generative adversarial networks (GANs) in 2014 marked a turning point in the field of generative AI. GANs consist of two neural networks, a generator and a discriminator, that compete against each other to generate realistic data. This adversarial training process has proven highly effective for creating images, videos, and other types of content.

The rise of transformers, a type of neural network architecture, has also had a profound impact on generative AI. Transformers excel at processing sequential data, such as text and audio, and have enabled the development of large language models with remarkable generative capabilities. The increasing availability of powerful computing hardware, such as GPUs (graphics processing units), has been essential for training large generative AI models. GPUs provide the computational power necessary to process massive datasets and perform complex calculations.

The exponential growth of data availability, fueled by the internet and the proliferation of digital devices, has provided generative AI models with the raw material they need to learn and generate realistic content. This combination of advancements helped generate AI to what it is today.

Future trends and potential advancements in generative AI technology.

Looking ahead, the future of generative AI technology holds immense promise, with potential advancements poised to transform various aspects of society, including mental healthcare. Several emerging trends and potential breakthroughs could shape the future of generative AI in the coming years. One promising trend is the development of more efficient and sustainable AI algorithms. Researchers are exploring techniques to reduce the computational resources required to train and deploy generative AI models, making them more accessible and environmentally friendly.

Another trend is the development of more explainable and transparent AI systems. As AI becomes more integrated into our lives, it is crucial to understand how these systems make decisions. Researchers are working on techniques to make generative AI models more transparent and explainable, allowing users to understand the reasoning behind their outputs. The integration of generative AI with other technologies, such as virtual reality and augmented reality, could unlock new possibilities for mental healthcare. Imagine virtual therapy sessions where AI-powered avatars provide personalized support and guidance in immersive environments. These new technological advancements are going to change the landscape of Generative AI.

The Ethical Landscape of AI in Mental Health

Privacy and Data Security: Safeguarding Sensitive Information

The importance of data privacy and security in mental healthcare.

As AI becomes increasingly integrated into mental healthcare, the ethical considerations surrounding its use demand careful attention. Among the most pressing concerns are those related to privacy and data security. Safeguarding sensitive patient information is not just a legal obligation but a moral imperative, essential for maintaining trust and ensuring responsible innovation.

Mental health data is particularly sensitive, encompassing deeply personal information about individuals' thoughts, emotions, behaviors, and experiences. This data can include details about diagnoses, treatment plans, medication history, therapy sessions, and personal relationships.

The potential for misuse or unauthorized access to this data raises serious ethical concerns. If patient data is not properly protected, it could be vulnerable to breaches, theft, or inappropriate disclosure. Such breaches can have devastating consequences for individuals, leading to discrimination, social stigma, and emotional distress. Moreover, the use of AI in mental healthcare often involves collecting and analyzing vast amounts of data, raising concerns about data aggregation and profiling.

If AI systems are trained on biased data, they could perpetuate or amplify existing inequalities, leading to unfair or discriminatory outcomes. For example, an AI-powered diagnostic tool trained on data primarily from one demographic group may not accurately diagnose individuals from other groups. Protecting this sensitive data is key to ensuring that patients feel secure.

Potential risks associated with using AI in mental health: data breaches, misuse of information.

The integration of AI in mental healthcare, while offering tremendous potential, introduces significant risks to patient privacy and data security. These risks stem from the inherent vulnerabilities of digital systems and the sensitive nature of the information being processed. Understanding these potential threats is crucial for implementing effective safeguards and mitigating potential harm. Data breaches represent a major concern. AI systems often rely on large datasets of patient information, which can be stored in centralized databases or cloud-based platforms. These databases can be attractive targets for hackers and cybercriminals seeking to steal sensitive information for financial gain or malicious purposes. A successful data breach can expose thousands or even millions of patient records, leading to identity theft, financial fraud, and emotional distress.

Even without malicious intent, the misuse of patient information poses a significant risk. AI algorithms can be used to analyze patient data for purposes other than direct clinical care, such as research, marketing, or insurance underwriting. If not properly regulated, such uses can lead to discrimination, unfair treatment, or violations of privacy. For example, insurance companies could use AI to identify individuals at risk for mental health conditions and deny them coverage or charge them higher premiums.

26

The use of AI in mental healthcare raises concerns about data sharing and third-party access. AI systems often rely on third-party vendors for data storage, processing, and analytics. These vendors may have access to patient data and could potentially use it for their own purposes. It is essential to ensure that these vendors adhere to strict privacy and security standards and are accountable for protecting patient information. The integration of AI needs to be approached with the knowledge of these issues.

Strategies for protecting patient privacy and ensuring data security: anonymization, encryption, compliance with regulations (e.g., HIPAA).

Protecting patient privacy and ensuring data security in the age of AI requires a multi-faceted approach, encompassing technological safeguards, policy frameworks, and ethical guidelines. Implementing robust strategies for anonymization, encryption, and regulatory compliance is essential for mitigating the risks associated with AI in mental healthcare. Anonymization techniques, such as de-identification and pseudonymization, play a crucial role in protecting patient privacy. De-identification involves removing or altering identifying information from patient records, such as names, addresses, and dates of birth. Pseudonymization replaces identifying information with pseudonyms or codes, making it more difficult to link data back to specific individuals. These techniques can help to reduce the risk of data breaches and misuse, while still allowing researchers to analyze patient data for valuable insights.

Encryption is another essential tool for safeguarding sensitive information. Encryption algorithms transform data into an unreadable format, making it unintelligible to unauthorized users. Encrypting patient data both in transit and at rest can help to prevent data breaches and protect against unauthorized access. Compliance with relevant regulations, such as the Health Insurance Portability and Accountability Act (HIPAA) in the United States, is crucial for ensuring that AI systems adhere to established privacy and security standards. HIPAA sets forth specific requirements for protecting patient health information, including rules regarding data security, privacy, and breach notification. Organizations that use AI in mental healthcare must comply with HIPAA regulations to avoid penalties and maintain patient trust.

In addition to these technical and legal measures, ethical guidelines play a vital role in promoting responsible AI practices. These guidelines should emphasize the importance of transparency, accountability, and fairness in the design and deployment of AI systems. They should also address issues such as data ownership, data consent, and the potential for bias in AI algorithms. Incorporating these strategies is key to protecting the sensitive information of patients.

Bias and Fairness: Ensuring Equitable Access and Outcomes
Understanding the concept of bias in AI models and its potential impact on mental health outcomes.

Bias in AI models represents a significant ethical challenge, particularly within the sensitive domain of mental healthcare. Understanding the nature and potential impact of bias is crucial for ensuring equitable access and positive outcomes for all individuals. AI models are trained on data, and if that data reflects existing societal biases, the models will inevitably learn and perpetuate those biases, leading to unfair or discriminatory results. Bias in AI can manifest in various forms, including algorithmic bias, data bias, and human bias. Algorithmic bias refers to biases that are inherent in the design or implementation of AI algorithms themselves. These biases can arise from the choice of algorithms, the way data is pre-processed, or the way the model is evaluated.

Data bias occurs when the training data used to develop AI models is not representative of the population to which the model will be applied. For example, if an AI-powered diagnostic tool for depression is trained primarily on data from white, middle-class individuals, it may not accurately diagnose depression in individuals from other racial, ethnic, or socioeconomic groups. Human bias can also influence AI models. Human bias can creep in at every stage of the AI lifecycle, from data collection and labeling to model development and deployment. Even seemingly objective decisions, such as choosing which features to include in a model or setting thresholds for diagnosis, can be influenced by human biases.

The potential impact of bias on mental health outcomes is far-reaching. Biased AI models can lead to misdiagnosis, inappropriate treatment recommendations, and unequal access to care. For example, a biased AI-powered chatbot may provide less effective support to individuals from marginalized communities, reinforcing existing inequalities in mental healthcare. Recognizing and addressing bias in AI is not merely a technical challenge but a moral imperative.

Sources of bias in AI datasets and algorithms: historical data, cultural biases, representation issues.

Identifying the sources of bias in AI datasets and algorithms is a critical step toward mitigating their harmful effects. Bias can creep into AI systems from various sources, including historical data, cultural biases, and representation issues within the data itself. Understanding these origins allows for more targeted and effective interventions to promote fairness and equity. Historical data often reflects past societal biases and inequalities, which can be perpetuated when used to train AI models. For example, if historical data shows that women are less likely to be diagnosed with certain mental health conditions than men, an AI model trained on this data may perpetuate this bias by underdiagnosing women with those conditions.

Cultural biases can also influence AI systems, particularly in the context of mental healthcare. Different cultures have different beliefs, values, and norms surrounding mental health, which can affect how mental health conditions are perceived, diagnosed, and treated. If AI models are trained on data that reflects only one cultural perspective, they may not be appropriate for use in other cultural contexts. Representation issues within AI datasets can also lead to bias. If certain demographic groups are underrepresented or overrepresented in the training data, the resulting AI model may not accurately reflect the characteristics of the broader population.

For example, if an AI-powered chatbot is trained primarily on data from English-speaking individuals, it may not be effective for individuals who speak other languages. The complexities of these biases require a multi-faceted approach for managing the AI fairly and equitably. Understanding how these issues can affect people is critical to preventing harm.

Strategies for mitigating bias and promoting fairness in AI-driven mental healthcare.

Mitigating bias and promoting fairness in AI-driven mental healthcare requires a proactive and multi-faceted approach, encompassing data diversity, algorithmic transparency, and ongoing monitoring and evaluation. Implementing these strategies is essential for ensuring equitable access to care and positive outcomes for all individuals, regardless of their background or circumstances. One of the most crucial steps is to ensure that AI datasets are diverse and representative of the populations they will be used to serve. This involves actively seeking out data from underrepresented groups and addressing any imbalances in the training data. Data augmentation techniques can also be used to increase the size and diversity of datasets, for example, by generating synthetic data that reflects the characteristics of underrepresented groups.

Algorithmic transparency is another important strategy for mitigating bias. This involves making the inner workings of AI algorithms more understandable and interpretable. Explainable AI (XAI) techniques can be used to shed light on how AI models make decisions, allowing developers and users to identify and address potential biases. Ongoing monitoring and evaluation are essential for detecting and addressing bias in AI systems over time. This involves regularly assessing the performance of AI models across different demographic groups and monitoring for any signs of unfair or discriminatory outcomes.

Feedback mechanisms should also be implemented to allow users to report potential biases or errors in AI systems. By incorporating diverse perspectives, promoting transparency, and continuously monitoring for bias, we can strive to create AI-driven mental healthcare systems that are fair, equitable, and beneficial for all. Working to improve the AI systems can help create more fairness and lessen bias.

Transparency and Explainability: Understanding AI Decision-Making
The need for transparency and explainability in AI systems used in mental healthcare.

The integration of AI into mental healthcare necessitates a commitment to transparency and explainability in AI systems. The opacity of many AI algorithms, often referred to as the "black box"

30

problem, poses significant ethical and practical challenges, particularly in high-stakes domains like mental health. Understanding why an AI system makes a particular decision is crucial for building trust, ensuring accountability, and promoting responsible innovation. Transparency refers to the degree to which the inner workings of an AI system are open and understandable. A transparent AI system allows users to see how data is processed, how decisions are made, and what factors influenced the outcome.

Explainability, on the other hand, refers to the ability to provide clear and concise explanations for why an AI system made a particular decision. An explainable AI system can justify its recommendations in a way that is understandable to both experts and non-experts. In mental healthcare, transparency and explainability are particularly important because AI systems are often used to make critical decisions that can have a profound impact on individuals' lives. For example, an AI-powered diagnostic tool may be used to diagnose a patient with a mental health condition, or an AI-driven chatbot may be used to provide therapeutic support.

In these situations, it is essential to understand how the AI system arrived at its conclusions and what factors were taken into consideration. This understanding is vital for building trust in the AI system, ensuring accountability for its decisions, and identifying and addressing potential biases or errors. Without transparency and explainability, AI systems risk becoming opaque and unaccountable, undermining their potential to improve mental healthcare.

Challenges in understanding how AI models make decisions: the "black box" problem.

One of the most significant challenges in the field of AI is the difficulty in understanding how complex models arrive at their decisions, a phenomenon often referred to as the "black box" problem. This opacity stems from the intricate nature of many AI algorithms, particularly deep learning models, which can involve millions or even billions of interconnected parameters. Deciphering the precise relationships between inputs and outputs in these models is a daunting task, hindering efforts to ensure transparency and accountability. The black box problem poses significant challenges in mental healthcare, where AI systems are increasingly used to support critical decisions. Clinicians need to understand how AI models arrive at their conclusions to assess their validity, identify potential biases, and make informed judgments about patient care.

Patients, the same way, need to understand how AI systems are being used to support their treatment and have the opportunity to challenge or question those decisions. Without transparency, it can be difficult to build trust in AI systems and ensure that they are used ethically and responsibly. The complexity of AI models can also make it difficult to identify and correct errors. If an AI system makes a mistake, it can be challenging to determine the root cause of the error and implement corrective measures. This is particularly concerning in mental healthcare, where errors can have serious consequences for patients' well-being.

The black box problem is not insurmountable. Researchers are actively developing techniques to make AI models more transparent and explainable. These techniques, often referred to as Explainable AI (XAI), aim to provide insights into the inner workings of AI systems, allowing users to understand how decisions are made and what factors were taken into consideration. Addressing this black box problem is vital to adopting AI across mental health care.

Approaches to improving transparency and explainability: explainable AI (XAI) techniques, model interpretability.

Addressing the "black box" problem and fostering greater transparency and explainability in AI systems requires a concerted effort to develop and implement innovative techniques. Explainable AI (XAI) encompasses a range of methods designed to shed light on the inner workings of AI models, making their decision-making processes more understandable and interpretable. Model interpretability, a key component of XAI, focuses on developing AI models that are inherently transparent and easy to understand. This can involve using simpler algorithms, limiting the complexity of the model, or designing models that explicitly reveal their reasoning process.

Various XAI techniques can be applied to improve transparency and explainability in AI systems used in mental healthcare. One approach is to use feature importance analysis to identify the factors that have the greatest influence on the model's predictions. This can help clinicians understand which aspects of a patient's data are most important in determining their diagnosis or treatment plan. Another technique involves generating counterfactual explanations, which provide insights into how the model's predictions would change if certain inputs were altered. This can help patients understand how their behavior or circumstances might affect their mental health outcomes.

Visualization techniques can be used to create graphical representations of the model's decision-making process. These visualizations can help clinicians and patients gain a more intuitive understanding of how the AI system works and what factors it considers. By employing these techniques, AI can be safely used to make a difference in mental health care. As more AI programs become more widely used it's essential to also increase the level of transparency that is provided.

AI-Powered Chatbots and Virtual Assistants: Personalized Support and Engagement

The Rise of AI Chatbots: Revolutionizing Mental Health Support

Introduction to AI-powered chatbots and their potential benefits in mental healthcare.

Artificial intelligence-powered chatbots and virtual assistants are emerging as transformative tools, poised to revolutionize mental health support and engagement. These interactive systems offer a unique opportunity to provide personalized, accessible, and on-demand care, addressing many of the limitations of traditional approaches. Understanding the potential benefits of AI chatbots is crucial for harnessing their power to improve mental wellbeing. At their core, AI chatbots are computer programs designed to simulate conversation with human users. They leverage natural language processing (NLP) and machine learning (ML) techniques to understand user input, generate appropriate responses, and engage in meaningful dialogue.

In the context of mental healthcare, AI chatbots can provide a range of services, including emotional support, psychoeducation, and guidance on coping strategies. They can also be used to monitor mood, track progress, and provide personalized reminders for medication or therapy appointments. The potential benefits of AI chatbots in mental healthcare are numerous. They offer 24/7 availability, providing individuals with support whenever and wherever they need it. This is particularly valuable for those experiencing acute mental health crises or who have difficulty accessing traditional services during regular business hours.

AI chatbots can also provide a high degree of anonymity, which may be appealing to individuals who are hesitant to seek help due to stigma or fear of judgment. The scalability of AI chatbots allows them to reach a large number of people at a relatively low cost, making them a particularly attractive option for addressing the growing demand for mental health services. Understanding the capabilities of AI chatbots is an important element of providing better access to mental healthcare. Overview of existing AI chatbot platforms for mental health: Woebot, Replika, etc.

The burgeoning field of AI-powered mental health support is exemplified by a growing number of innovative chatbot platforms designed to provide accessible and engaging care. These platforms leverage the power of natural language processing and machine learning to offer a range of services, from emotional support and psychoeducation to guided interventions and personalized monitoring. Examining some of the leading examples provides valuable insights into the current state of the art and the potential for future advancements. Woebot is one of the most well-known and widely used AI chatbot platforms for mental health. Woebot delivers cognitive behavioral therapy (CBT) techniques through a conversational interface, helping users identify and challenge negative thought patterns. It also provides mood tracking, personalized insights, and coping strategies for managing stress and anxiety.

Replika takes a different approach, focusing on creating a personalized AI companion that can provide emotional support and companionship. Replika users can customize their AI friend's personality, appearance, and interests, creating a unique and supportive relationship. The platform aims to reduce feelings of loneliness and isolation, offering a safe space for users to express their thoughts and feelings without judgment. Other platforms, such as Youper and Talkspace, offer a combination of AI-powered support and access to licensed therapists. These platforms use AI to screen users, provide initial assessments, and match them with therapists who are a good fit.

These chatbot platforms provide a valuable, often more accessible and less costly, alternative to traditional methods of therapy. It should be understood that these are not replacements for mental health professionals, but another tool that can be used to get support. The existing platforms continue to adapt and improve with the rapid pace of AI improvements.

How chatbots can provide personalized support: emotional validation, CBT-based interventions, mindfulness exercises.

The effectiveness of AI-powered chatbots in mental healthcare lies in their ability to provide personalized support tailored to individual needs and preferences. Through natural language processing and machine learning, these chatbots can adapt to users' unique circumstances, providing emotional validation, delivering CBT-based interventions, and guiding them through mindfulness exercises. Emotional validation is a crucial component of mental health support, and AI chatbots can be programmed to recognize and respond to users' emotions with empathy and understanding. By acknowledging and validating users' feelings, chatbots can create a sense of connection and support, encouraging them to open up and share their experiences. This can be particularly helpful for individuals who may feel hesitant to express their emotions to others due to stigma or fear of judgment.

AI chatbots can also be used to deliver CBT-based interventions, helping users identify and challenge negative thought patterns and behaviors. Through interactive exercises and guided prompts, chatbots can help users develop healthier coping mechanisms and improve their overall mental wellbeing. These interventions can be tailored to address specific issues, such as anxiety, depression, or stress. Mindfulness exercises are another valuable tool for promoting mental wellbeing, and AI chatbots can guide users through various mindfulness practices, such as meditation, deep breathing, and body scan techniques. These exercises can help users cultivate present moment awareness, reduce stress, and improve their overall sense of calm and wellbeing.

These personalization tactics are vital in making sure that mental health patients are getting quality support and guidance. The adaptability and personalization are key to getting positive outcomes. The accessibility also allows these chatbots to assist more people who may not otherwise have access to care.

Enhancing Engagement and Adherence: Gamification and Personalized Reminders

Using AI to improve engagement and adherence to mental health treatment plans.

A significant challenge in mental healthcare is ensuring that individuals actively engage with their treatment plans and adhere to recommended interventions. AI offers promising solutions for enhancing engagement and adherence through gamification techniques and personalized reminders, making the treatment process more interactive, rewarding, and convenient. Traditional mental health treatment plans often require individuals to actively participate in therapy sessions, take medication as prescribed, and practice coping strategies on their own. However, many individuals struggle to maintain consistent engagement and adherence, leading to suboptimal outcomes. Factors such as lack of motivation, forgetfulness, and practical challenges can all contribute to non-adherence.

Gamification involves incorporating game-like elements into the treatment process to make it more engaging and enjoyable. This can include earning points, badges, or rewards for completing tasks, participating in challenges, and achieving goals. AI-powered chatbots can be used to gamify mental health treatment plans by providing personalized challenges, tracking progress, and offering virtual rewards for completing activities. Personalized reminders are another effective way to improve adherence to mental health treatment plans. AI chatbots can send timely and relevant reminders to individuals, reminding them to take their medication, attend therapy appointments, or practice coping strategies.

These reminders can be tailored to individual preferences and needs, taking into account factors such as the individual's schedule, preferred communication channel, and past adherence patterns. By making treatment plans more engaging, rewarding, and convenient, AI has the potential to significantly improve engagement and adherence, leading to better mental health outcomes. The personalization and accessibility also allow individuals to stay more engaged and on-track for getting the care they need.

Gamification techniques: rewards, challenges, and progress tracking.

Gamification techniques represent a powerful toolkit for enhancing engagement and adherence in AI-driven mental health interventions. By incorporating elements of game design, these techniques transform traditionally mundane or challenging tasks into more interactive, rewarding, and enjoyable experiences. Rewards, challenges, and progress tracking are core components of gamification, each contributing to increased motivation and sustained participation. Rewards can take many forms, ranging from virtual badges and points to access to exclusive content or features. These rewards provide tangible recognition of individuals' efforts and accomplishments, reinforcing positive behaviors and encouraging continued engagement.

Challenges add an element of excitement and competition to the treatment process. AI-powered chatbots can present users with personalized challenges tailored to their specific needs and goals. These challenges can range from completing daily mindfulness exercises to tracking mood for a week or engaging in social activities. Progress tracking provides individuals with a visual representation of their achievements and milestones. AI chatbots can track various metrics, such as mood scores, therapy session attendance, and medication adherence, displaying progress in a clear and motivating way.

The sense of accomplishment that comes with seeing progress can be a powerful motivator for individuals to continue working toward their goals. Gamification can be a fun and engaging method for patients to stay on track with getting better. Using it in conjunction with standard practices can provide a new way to engage with treatment. All of these rewards and challenges are able to keep clients motivated.

Personalized reminders and notifications: medication adherence, appointment reminders.

Personalized reminders and notifications, powered by AI, represent a simple yet highly effective strategy for improving adherence to mental health treatment plans. By delivering timely and relevant reminders, these systems help individuals stay on track with their medication schedules, therapy appointments, and self-care activities. Medication adherence is a critical aspect of managing many mental health conditions, and AI-powered reminders can play a vital role in ensuring that individuals take their medication as prescribed. These reminders can be tailored to individual schedules and preferences, taking into account factors such as the time of day, preferred communication channel, and past adherence patterns.

Appointment reminders are equally important for ensuring that individuals attend their therapy sessions and other healthcare appointments. AI chatbots can send automated reminders via text message, email, or push notification, reducing the likelihood of missed appointments. These reminders can also include helpful information, such as the date, time, and location of the appointment, as well as any instructions or preparation required. Going beyond just medication and appointments, reminders can also be used to facilitate self-care activities.

AI can also be used to provide reminders for self-care activities, such as exercise, mindfulness practice, or social engagement. These reminders can be tailored to individual needs and preferences, encouraging individuals to prioritize their mental wellbeing. These AI-powered prompts can ensure that clients stay on track to getting the support and treatment they need. This approach also makes it easier for people to schedule, because reminders can easily be set and followed.

Real-World Examples and Case Studies: Successes and Limitations
Case studies of successful AI chatbot implementations in mental healthcare settings.

The theoretical potential of AI chatbots in mental healthcare is increasingly supported by real-world examples and case studies demonstrating their effectiveness in various settings. These implementations showcase the ability of AI to enhance access, personalize support, and improve outcomes for individuals facing mental health challenges. Analyzing these successes provides valuable insights into best practices and areas for further innovation. One notable example is the use of Woebot in a study published in the Journal of Medical Internet Research. The study found that Woebot was effective in reducing symptoms of depression and anxiety in young adults. Participants who used Woebot reported significant improvements in their mood and overall wellbeing compared to a control group.

Another case study involves the use of an AI chatbot to provide support to individuals with substance use disorders. The chatbot, named " □□□□ " (Shahosh), offers personalized coping strategies, relapse prevention techniques, and links to local resources. A pilot study found that users of " □□□□ " reported increased self-efficacy and reduced cravings compared to those receiving traditional treatment. These show how technology can be used to help combat substance abuse. Other successful implementations of AI chatbots include their use in providing support to frontline healthcare workers during the COVID-19 pandemic and in delivering mental health services to college students.

These are examples of cases where AI is being used to create better access and options for people needing mental healthcare. While these case studies are promising, it's important to note that AI is still fairly new and it's important to continue to monitor and test the results. It's also vital to continue innovating and finding better ways to get support to those in need.

Limitations of AI chatbots: lack of empathy, inability to handle complex situations, potential for misinterpretation.

Despite the promising successes of AI chatbots in mental healthcare, it's crucial to acknowledge their inherent limitations. These limitations stem from the fundamental differences between human and artificial intelligence, impacting the ability of chatbots to provide truly empathetic support, effectively handle complex situations, and avoid potential misinterpretations. One of the most significant limitations is the lack of genuine empathy. While AI chatbots can be programmed to recognize and respond to emotions, they cannot truly feel or understand human emotions in the same way that a human therapist can. Empathy requires a deep level of understanding, compassion, and shared experience that is currently beyond the capabilities of AI.

This lack of empathy can make it difficult for chatbots to provide truly meaningful support, particularly in situations where individuals are experiencing intense emotional distress. AI chatbots also struggle to handle complex or nuanced situations that require critical thinking, creativity, and judgment. These bots are limited by their training data and programming, unable to deviate from pre-defined scripts or adapt to unexpected circumstances. This can make them ineffective in dealing with individuals with complex mental health conditions or those experiencing unique or unusual challenges.

The potential for misinterpretation is another concern. AI chatbots rely on natural language processing to understand user input, and even the most sophisticated NLP algorithms are not perfect. Chatbots can misinterpret user statements, misunderstand their intent, or provide inaccurate or inappropriate responses. This is particularly problematic in mental healthcare, where misinterpretations can have serious consequences. These limitations are important to remember as people explore using AI for their mental health. These limitations help show that these AI programs are helpful, but are not a replacement for human care.

Future directions for AI chatbot development: improved natural language processing, enhanced emotional intelligence.

The limitations of current AI chatbots highlight the need for continued research and development to improve their capabilities and address their shortcomings. Future directions for AI chatbot development focus on enhancing natural language processing (NLP) and cultivating emotional intelligence, paving the way for more effective and empathetic support. Improved NLP is crucial for enabling chatbots to better understand user input, interpret nuances in language, and avoid misinterpretations. Researchers are exploring various techniques to enhance NLP, including developing more sophisticated algorithms, incorporating contextual information, and training models on larger and more diverse datasets.

These advancements will allow chatbots to engage in more natural and meaningful conversations, providing users with more relevant and helpful responses. Cultivating emotional intelligence is another key area of focus. Researchers are exploring ways to equip chatbots with the ability to recognize, understand, and respond to human emotions with greater sensitivity and empathy. This involves developing algorithms that can detect subtle cues in user language, facial expressions, and tone of voice, as well as programming chatbots to respond with appropriate emotional support and validation.

This will allow chatbots to build stronger relationships with users, fostering trust and creating a more supportive therapeutic environment. The ongoing efforts to improve NLP and develop emotional intelligence will allow AI to be even more helpful. As AI advances, chatbots have the potential to become invaluable tools for enhancing access to and improving the quality of mental healthcare.

AI for Diagnosis and Assessment: Early Detection and Personalized Treatment

Leveraging AI for Early Detection of Mental Health Conditions

The importance of early detection in improving mental health outcomes.

Early detection is paramount in improving mental health outcomes, allowing for timely intervention and preventing the escalation of mental health conditions. AI offers innovative tools for early detection, analyzing vast amounts of data to identify individuals at risk and facilitate prompt access to appropriate care. The consequences of untreated mental illness can be devastating, impacting individuals' relationships, careers, and overall quality of life. Early detection allows for interventions to be implemented before mental health conditions become severe or chronic, improving the likelihood of successful treatment and recovery. It can also help to prevent secondary problems, such as substance abuse, homelessness, and suicide.

Traditional methods of mental health screening often rely on self-report questionnaires or clinical interviews, which can be time-consuming, expensive, and subject to biases. AI offers a more efficient and objective approach, analyzing data from various sources to identify individuals at risk. This data can include medical records, social media activity, wearable sensor data, and even speech patterns. By identifying individuals at risk early on, AI can facilitate prompt access to appropriate care, such as therapy, medication, or support groups.

This can lead to better outcomes, reduced healthcare costs, and improved overall wellbeing. In addition to improving individual outcomes, early detection can also have a positive impact on public health. By identifying individuals at risk and providing them with early intervention, AI can help to reduce the overall burden of mental illness in society. This is an important tool for getting better mental health outcomes across society. Having AI tools for early detection can lead to the lives of patients improving in the long term.

How AI can analyze data to identify early warning signs of mental health conditions: sentiment analysis, social media monitoring.

AI's ability to sift through vast datasets and discern subtle patterns makes it uniquely suited for identifying early warning signs of mental health conditions. Through techniques like sentiment analysis and social media monitoring, AI can detect changes in behavior, language, and emotional expression that may indicate an individual is at risk. Sentiment analysis utilizes natural language processing (NLP) to assess the emotional tone or sentiment expressed in text. By analyzing social media posts, online forums, and other forms of digital communication, AI can detect shifts in sentiment that may indicate a decline in mental wellbeing. For example, a sudden increase in negative emotions, such as sadness, anger, or anxiety, could be a warning sign of depression or another mental health condition.

Social media monitoring involves using AI to track an individual's online activity, identifying changes in their behavior, social interactions, and expressed interests. This can include monitoring the frequency and content of their posts, the types of groups they join, and the topics they discuss. Changes in these patterns can provide valuable insights into their mental state. For example, a sudden decrease in social activity, a shift towards more negative or isolating content, or an expression of suicidal thoughts could all be warning signs of a mental health crisis.

It is important to note that the use of sentiment analysis and social media monitoring for early detection of mental health conditions raises significant ethical considerations regarding privacy and data security. It is essential to implement appropriate safeguards to protect individuals' privacy and ensure that data is used responsibly and ethically. Using this data must be balanced to protect the individual. The use of AI should be used for good and for helping people get the care they need.

Examples of AI-driven tools for early detection: predictive models, risk assessment algorithms.

The application of AI in early mental health detection is manifested through various innovative tools, including predictive models and risk assessment algorithms. These tools leverage machine learning to analyze data and identify individuals at heightened risk of developing or experiencing a mental health crisis, allowing for proactive intervention. Predictive models employ statistical algorithms to forecast the likelihood of future events based on historical data. In mental healthcare, these models can analyze patient records, demographic information, and other relevant data to predict the probability of an individual developing a mental health condition.

By identifying those at high risk, healthcare providers can prioritize early intervention efforts, such as screening, counseling, or medication. Risk assessment algorithms, similarly, assess an individual's current risk level based on specific factors and indicators. These algorithms can analyze data from various sources, such as self-report questionnaires, clinical interviews, and behavioral observations, to identify individuals who are experiencing acute mental health crises or are at risk of suicide.

These tools enable healthcare professionals to make more informed decisions about treatment planning and resource allocation. Using these tools proactively can improve treatment outcomes and also help prevent tragic events. These tools also allow more people to have access to quick and efficient assessments that may not otherwise be available to them. These advances are important for getting people the care they need.

Using AI to personalize mental health treatment plans based on individual patient characteristics.

Moving beyond early detection, AI has the power to revolutionize treatment planning by tailoring interventions to individual patient characteristics. This personalized approach recognizes that each individual is unique, and what works for one person may not work for another. AI algorithms can analyze vast amounts of patient data, including genetic information, medical history, lifestyle factors, and personal preferences, to identify the most effective treatment strategies for each individual. Traditional treatment planning often relies on a one-size-fits-all approach, with patients being assigned to standardized treatment protocols based on their diagnosis.

However, this approach can be inefficient and ineffective, as it fails to account for the individual variations that can influence treatment outcomes. AI-powered personalized treatment planning offers a more precise and targeted approach, taking into account the complex interplay of factors that contribute to mental health conditions. By identifying the specific characteristics that are most relevant to an individual's treatment response, AI can help clinicians select the most appropriate interventions, optimize medication dosages, and develop personalized coping strategies.

This can lead to improved treatment outcomes, reduced side effects, and increased patient satisfaction. Additionally, this approach can help cut down on the cost and time that is associated with less personalized treatment plans. With AI, the ability to plan treatments and make decisions can be made more efficient and impactful. This is key to maximizing the ability of the patient to recover and move forward.

Factors to consider when personalizing treatment: genetics, lifestyle, personal preferences.

Effective personalization of mental health treatment plans

hinges on a comprehensive understanding of the individual, encompassing genetic predispositions, lifestyle factors, and personal preferences. AI algorithms can analyze these diverse data points to create a holistic profile of each patient, enabling clinicians to tailor interventions with unprecedented precision. Genetics plays a significant role in mental health, with certain genes increasing the risk for specific conditions. AI can analyze an individual's genetic makeup to identify potential vulnerabilities and inform treatment decisions. For example, pharmacogenomics testing can be used to determine how an individual is likely to respond to different medications, helping to avoid ineffective treatments and minimize side effects.

Lifestyle factors, such as diet, exercise, sleep patterns, and social connections, also have a profound impact on mental wellbeing. AI can analyze data from wearable sensors, mobile apps, and social media to track an individual's lifestyle habits and identify areas for improvement. This information can be used to develop personalized recommendations for lifestyle changes that can support mental health. Understanding an individual's personal preferences is crucial for creating a treatment plan that they are likely to adhere to. AI can gather information about an individual's values, interests, and coping styles through questionnaires, interviews, and behavioral observations.

This information can be used to select treatment modalities, therapeutic techniques, and self-care activities that align with their personal preferences. By considering these various factors, clinicians are better equipped to plan care that suits each individual. AI is then leveraged to analyze those factors efficiently. These personalized approached are key to getting positive outcomes.

Examples of AI-driven tools for personalized treatment planning: machine learning algorithms, decision support systems.

The promise of personalized treatment planning in mental healthcare is being realized through the development and deployment of various AI-driven tools, including machine learning algorithms and clinical decision support systems. These tools leverage data analysis and predictive modeling to assist clinicians in making more informed and individualized treatment decisions. Machine learning algorithms can

49

analyze vast amounts of patient data to identify patterns and predict treatment outcomes. These algorithms can be trained on historical data from clinical trials and real-world practice to identify the factors that are most strongly associated with treatment success.

The algorithms can then be used to predict which treatment is most likely to be effective for a new patient based on their individual characteristics. Clinical decision support systems (CDSSs) integrate AI algorithms with clinical knowledge and best practice guidelines to provide clinicians with real-time recommendations and guidance. These systems can analyze patient data, identify potential drug interactions, suggest appropriate dosages, and provide alerts about potential risks or side effects. They act as a virtual assistant, providing immediate actionable items.

CDSSs are being integrated into electronic health records (EHRs), providing clinicians with seamless access to personalized treatment recommendations at the point of care. By leveraging these AI-driven tools, clinicians can make more informed decisions about treatment planning, improve patient outcomes, and reduce the risk of errors. These systems can give the provider better and more complete information that results in better overall care. AI is an invaluable tool for treatment planning.

AI-Assisted Therapy: Enhancing Traditional Therapeutic Approaches
How AI can enhance traditional therapy models: providing real-time feedback, identifying patterns in patient behavior.

Beyond diagnosis and treatment planning, AI offers exciting possibilities for enhancing traditional therapy models, augmenting the capabilities of therapists and improving patient outcomes. AI can act as a virtual assistant, providing real-time feedback to therapists during sessions and identifying subtle patterns in patient behavior that might otherwise be missed. Real-time feedback can be invaluable for therapists, helping them to tailor their approach and maximize the effectiveness of each session. AI algorithms can analyze patient language, tone of voice, and facial expressions to detect emotional states, identify signs of distress, and assess the patient's level of engagement.

50

This information can be provided to the therapist in real-time, allowing them to adjust their communication style, explore specific topics in more depth, or provide additional support as needed. Identifying patterns in patient behavior is another area where AI can excel. By analyzing data from therapy sessions, wearable sensors, and mobile apps, AI can identify subtle patterns in a patient's behavior, mood, and cognitive functioning. These patterns can provide valuable insights into the patient's underlying mental health condition, helping therapists to develop more targeted and effective treatment strategies.

By providing real-time feedback and identifying patterns in patient behavior, AI can help therapists to deliver more personalized, effective, and evidence-based care. This can lead to improved patient outcomes, increased engagement, and a more satisfying therapeutic experience. With AI-assisted technology, providers are able to keep better track of the progress that their patients are making during treatment. These new tech tools can be invaluable and life-changing for many people.

Examples of AI-assisted therapy tools: virtual reality therapy, biofeedback systems.

The potential of AI-assisted therapy is being realized through the development and implementation of various innovative tools, including virtual reality (VR) therapy and biofeedback systems. These tools leverage technology to create immersive and engaging therapeutic experiences, augmenting traditional therapy models and expanding access to care. Virtual reality (VR) therapy uses computer-generated environments to simulate real-world scenarios, allowing patients to confront their fears and anxieties in a safe and controlled setting. VR therapy has shown promise in treating a range of mental health conditions, including anxiety disorders, phobias, post-traumatic stress disorder (PTSD), and social anxiety.

For example, individuals with social anxiety can practice social interactions in a virtual environment, gradually increasing their comfort level and confidence. Individuals with PTSD can re-experience traumatic events in a safe and controlled setting, processing their emotions and reducing their symptoms. Biofeedback systems use sensors to monitor physiological signals, such as heart rate, breathing patterns, and muscle tension, providing patients with real-time feedback about their bodily responses. This feedback allows patients to learn how to regulate their physiological responses and manage stress, anxiety, and pain.

AI algorithms can be integrated into biofeedback systems to provide personalized guidance and support. For example, an AI-powered biofeedback system can analyze a patient's physiological data to identify specific patterns of stress and provide personalized recommendations for relaxation techniques. These AI-assisted tools are able to add helpful technology to allow people to combat mental health issues. VR and biofeedback are tools that give providers other options for approaching care.

The role of therapists in the age of AI: collaboration and adaptation.

As AI becomes increasingly integrated into mental healthcare, the role of therapists is evolving, requiring a shift towards collaboration and adaptation. Rather than being replaced by AI, therapists will play a crucial role in guiding and overseeing the use of AI-assisted tools, ensuring that they are used ethically, effectively, and in a way that complements human connection and empathy. Therapists can leverage AI tools to enhance their practice, providing more personalized, evidence-based, and efficient care. They can use AI-powered diagnostic tools to identify individuals at risk, develop personalized treatment plans, and monitor patient progress.

They can also use AI-assisted therapy tools, such as virtual reality and biofeedback systems, to create more engaging and effective therapeutic experiences. It's important to remember that the human connection cannot be replicated by computers. As these new technology options are released it's critical that humans stay involved. This human element will help improve the quality of care, increase the likelihood of positive outcomes and prevent unethical practices.

This collaboration is key to making sure that patients get everything they need to improve their mental health. Therapists of the future need to be open and educated to use AI in conjunction with more traditional methods. This is not about replacing people, but about using AI to make their lives easier. The hope is that collaboration between AI and therapists leads to positive and long-lasting improvements in mental healthcare for all people.

Generative AI in Content Creation for Mental Wellbeing

AI-Generated Content for Mental Health Education

How AI can generate accessible and engaging content on mental health topics.

Generative AI presents an unprecedented opportunity to democratize mental health education by creating accessible and engaging content tailored to diverse audiences. Overcoming barriers of cost, language, and complexity, AI can generate a wealth of resources that empower individuals to understand, manage, and promote their mental wellbeing. Traditional mental health education often relies on static materials, such as brochures, websites, and lectures, which may not be engaging or accessible to everyone. Generative AI can create dynamic and interactive content that adapts to individual learning styles and preferences.

AI algorithms can generate text, images, audio, and video content that explains complex mental health concepts in a clear, concise, and engaging manner. This content can be tailored to specific age groups, cultural backgrounds, and literacy levels, ensuring that it is accessible to a wide range of individuals. By creating personalized content, AI can help to break down stigma, promote understanding, and encourage individuals to seek help when they need it. The cost of hiring specialists to create such content can be prohibitive, but AI offers an affordable alternative.

AI also can produce content in many different languages that allows it to be truly global and accessible. This is invaluable as there are many who may struggle or be unable to access mental health support in their own language. The versatility and adaptability of AI make it a unique tool for mental health education.

Examples of AI-generated content: articles, videos, infographics, and social media posts.

The power of generative AI in mental health education is readily apparent when considering the diverse range of content it can produce: from informative articles and engaging videos to visually appealing infographics and impactful social media posts. These various formats allow for tailored delivery of crucial information, reaching different audiences in ways that resonate most effectively. AI can generate articles that explain complex mental health topics in a clear and concise manner, providing readers with a deeper understanding of conditions, treatments, and coping strategies. These articles can be tailored to different reading levels and cultural backgrounds, ensuring that they are accessible to a wide range of individuals.

AI can also create engaging videos that illustrate mental health concepts in a visually appealing and memorable way. These videos can feature animations, real-life stories, and expert interviews, capturing viewers' attention and promoting understanding. For those who prefer visual learning, AI can generate infographics that present complex information in a clear and concise format. These infographics can use charts, graphs, and illustrations to highlight key statistics, summarize research findings, and provide practical tips for improving mental well-being.

The ability to create tailored content that can educate the public has never been more possible. From short social media snippets to longer more in-depth articles, Generative AI allows people to better understand mental health, so we can work to end stigma and ensure more people get the care that they need. These formats all have a significant influence on how information is conveyed.

Using AI to tailor content to specific audiences and cultural contexts.

One of the most significant advantages of using AI in mental health education is its ability to tailor content to specific audiences and cultural contexts, enhancing its relevance and impact. Traditional educational materials often take a one-size-fits-all approach, which may not resonate with individuals from diverse backgrounds or with varying needs. AI can analyze demographic data, cultural norms, and individual preferences to create content that is culturally sensitive, linguistically appropriate, and tailored to the specific needs of the target audience.

For example, AI can generate content that addresses the unique mental health challenges faced by specific age groups, such as adolescents, young adults, or seniors. It can also create content that reflects the cultural values and beliefs of different ethnic or religious groups, ensuring that the information is presented in a way that is respectful and relatable. Language is another important consideration. AI can automatically translate content into multiple languages, making it accessible to individuals who may not speak the dominant language. It can also adapt the language style and tone to suit the preferences of the target audience.

This is a monumental step forward as it allows many to gain knowledge of mental health in their own language, which can bring a greater understanding. AI also can help people from different cultural backgrounds relate to the issues in ways that make sense and are impactful to them. By tailoring content to specific audiences and cultural contexts, AI can help to break down barriers, promote understanding, and encourage individuals to seek help when they need it. This will have an impact on ending the stigma and helping to increase awareness.

Personalized Meditation and Mindfulness Programs
Creating personalized meditation and mindfulness programs using generative AI.

Generative AI unlocks the potential to create truly personalized meditation and mindfulness programs, catering to individual preferences, needs, and progress, thereby enhancing engagement and effectiveness. Moving beyond generic, pre-recorded sessions, AI can adapt the content, pace, and style of meditation and mindfulness exercises to suit each user's unique profile. This includes adapting programs to preferred meditation styles, like guided imagery, breathwork, or body scans. Some prefer certain guided meditations, and AI allows those to be specifically tailored and curated.

AI can also adjust the length and frequency of meditation sessions based on the user's schedule, availability, and progress. Short, mini-meditations can be incorporated into busy days, while longer sessions can be scheduled for times when the user has more time to relax. These adjustments can also factor in progress over time. The pacing can be increased or decreased, and suggestions and recommendations can be made based on that progress.

By incorporating these factors, it allows the users to have better control over the process. It also ensures that the practices are convenient, accessible, and something they can use. There is great power in having tailored and adaptable meditation practices to promote mental health. AI allows this to happen in very unique and customized ways.

Tailoring content based on individual needs, preferences, and progress.
The creation of truly effective personalized meditation and mindfulness programs through generative AI hinges on the ability to tailor content based on a deep understanding of individual needs, expressed preferences, and demonstrable progress over time. This dynamic adaptation ensures sustained engagement and maximizes the potential benefits of these practices. Addressing individual needs requires more than just a superficial understanding of demographic data. AI can analyze a user's mental health history, current stress levels, and specific challenges to create content that is directly relevant to their situation.

56

For example, someone struggling with anxiety might benefit from meditations focused on calming the nervous system, while someone dealing with grief might find solace in exercises centered on acceptance and self-compassion. Recognizing and responding to user preferences is also crucial. AI can learn a user's preferred voice, background music, and meditation style through feedback mechanisms and behavioral data. It can then generate content that aligns with these preferences, creating a more enjoyable and engaging experience. It can even learn what kind of guidance is more or less helpful and adapt the content accordingly.

Progress tracking is essential for ensuring that meditation and mindfulness programs are effective. AI can monitor a user's mood, stress levels, and sleep patterns to assess their progress over time. It can then adjust the difficulty and complexity of the exercises, providing gentle encouragement and support as needed. By dynamically adapting content to individual needs, preferences, and progress, AI ensures that meditation and mindfulness programs remain relevant, engaging, and effective. This type of adaptability is invaluable when managing mental health.

Examples of AI-powered meditation apps: Headspace, Calm.

While the full potential of generative AI in creating truly personalized meditation and mindfulness programs is still unfolding, existing AI-powered meditation apps like Headspace and Calm offer valuable examples of how technology is already being used to enhance these practices. These apps, while not fully utilizing generative AI in the sense of creating entirely new content on-the-fly, leverage AI algorithms for personalization, progress tracking, and adaptive content delivery. Headspace, a popular meditation app, uses AI to personalize the user experience by recommending specific meditation courses based on their goals, experience level, and mood.

The app also tracks user progress, providing insights into their meditation habits and offering personalized encouragement. Calm, another leading meditation app, uses AI to create personalized sleep stories and music playlists designed to promote relaxation and improve sleep quality. The app also offers a variety of guided meditations led

57

by experienced instructors, covering a wide range of topics and techniques. While these apps don't yet have the capability to generate entirely new meditations based on your individual data, they do offer a level of personalization and adaptation that was not possible before AI.

The algorithms are able to understand and customize the offerings so the users can gain the best support for their own mental health. This customization ensures that patients can be the most successful. By highlighting Headspace and Calm, it provides insight and support in a way that promotes healing and relaxation. These are good examples of what the future holds as this technology progresses.

AI in Creative Therapies: Art, Music, and Writing
Exploring the potential of AI in creative therapies: art, music, and writing.

Creative therapies, including art, music, and writing, have long been recognized for their ability to promote emotional expression, reduce stress, and enhance overall wellbeing. Generative AI opens up exciting new avenues for exploring the potential of these therapies, providing individuals with powerful tools to unlock their creativity and access their inner worlds. By assisting in the creation of art, music and written stories, it allows people to create more complex, professional pieces that can express more accurately how they are feeling. AI is able to assist individuals at any skill level, making this a truly accessible medium.

AI algorithms can generate unique art prompts, guiding individuals to explore specific emotions, themes, or memories through visual expression. These prompts can be tailored to individual needs and preferences, encouraging creativity and self-discovery. Those who may struggle with art, or don't see themselves as artists, may be more inclined to try if they know AI can help guide them. The same goes for music or creative writing, as these programs allow anyone to generate professional results that accurately portray the way they are feeling.

AI empowers individuals to express themselves, process their emotions, and connect with their inner creativity. While AI can't replace the connection from a therapist, it can become another tool to allow people to improve their lives. The accessibility of AI-driven art, music, and writing experiences can make creative therapies more widely available. This allows more people to benefit from expressing themselves.

Using AI to generate art, music, and writing prompts for therapeutic purposes.

The generation of targeted and evocative prompts forms a cornerstone of AI's utility in creative therapies, offering a catalyst for self-expression and emotional exploration through art, music, and writing. These AI-generated prompts can break down creative barriers, providing individuals with a starting point for their therapeutic journey and guiding them towards deeper self-discovery. In art therapy, AI can generate prompts that encourage individuals to explore specific emotions, memories, or themes through visual expression. For example, AI might generate prompts such as "draw a picture of your safe space," "create an abstract representation of your anxiety," or "paint a portrait of your inner child."

In music therapy, AI can generate musical prompts that encourage individuals to express their emotions through sound. For instance, AI could generate prompts such as "compose a melody that reflects your current mood," "create a soundscape that evokes feelings of peace and tranquility," or "write lyrics that express your hopes for the future." For writing therapy, the AI can generate text prompts that allow clients to express themselves or process emotions. These can be very specific, or more open ended to allow the client to drive the project forward.

These AI-generated prompts are not intended to replace the guidance of a trained therapist, but to supplement and enhance the therapeutic process. They provide a framework for creative exploration, helping individuals to overcome creative blocks and tap into their inner resources. AI can be used to provide the sparks needed to help people express themselves and heal. This technology provides endless opportunities.

AI in Creative Therapies: Art, Music, and Writing
Examples of AI-driven tools for creative expression.

The potential of AI in creative therapies is being realized through the development and increasing availability of various AI-driven tools designed to facilitate artistic expression in art, music, and writing. These tools empower individuals to explore their creativity, process their emotions, and connect with their inner worlds in new and engaging ways. Several AI-powered art generation tools, such as DALL-E 2, Midjourney, and Stable Diffusion, allow users to create stunning visuals from textual descriptions. These tools can be used to generate unique art therapy prompts, visualize personal experiences, or express emotions through abstract imagery.

For example, a user could input the prompt "a vibrant painting of my anxiety" and the AI would generate a unique image based on that description. AI music composition tools, such as Amper Music and Jukebox, enable users to create original music even without prior musical experience. These tools use AI algorithms to generate melodies, harmonies, and rhythms based on user input, allowing individuals to express their emotions and explore their creativity through sound. AI is changing the world and expanding creative practices to people.

AI writing assistants, such as GPT-3 and Sudowrite, can help users overcome writer's block, generate new ideas, and refine their writing style. These tools can be used to generate poetry, short stories, scripts, and other forms of creative writing. AI can provide support with grammar, style and flow allowing people to spend more time creating and expressing. There are very few limits to what these systems can accomplish. AI provides an opportunity for more people to dive into the creative world.

Addressing the Challenges: Overcoming Barriers to Adoption

Regulatory and Legal Considerations: Navigating the Complexities

Overview of relevant regulations and legal frameworks governing the use of AI in healthcare.

The integration of AI into mental healthcare, while holding immense potential, necessitates careful consideration of the regulatory and legal landscape. Navigating the complexities of these frameworks is crucial for ensuring responsible innovation, protecting patient rights, and fostering trust in AI-driven solutions. The use of AI in healthcare is subject to a variety of regulations and legal frameworks that vary depending on the jurisdiction and the specific application of AI. These regulations often address issues such as data privacy, data security, medical device regulation, and professional liability.

Data privacy regulations, such as the Health Insurance Portability and Accountability Act (HIPAA) in the United States and the General Data Protection Regulation (GDPR) in Europe, set forth strict requirements for protecting patient health information. These regulations govern the collection, use, storage, and disclosure of protected health information (PHI), including mental health data. Medical device regulations, such as those enforced by the Food and Drug Administration (FDA) in the United States, apply to AI-powered tools that are used for diagnosis, treatment, or prevention of disease. These regulations require that medical devices be safe, effective, and properly labeled.

Understanding the applicable regulations is essential for ensuring that AI systems are developed and deployed in compliance with the law and in a way that protects patient rights and promotes ethical practices. AI developers, healthcare providers, and policymakers must work together to create clear and consistent regulations that promote innovation while safeguarding patient well-being. This collaborative effort will lead to better outcomes for everyone.

Compliance with data privacy laws: GDPR, CCPA.

Data privacy laws, such as the General Data Protection Regulation (GDPR) and the California Consumer Privacy Act (CCPA), impose stringent requirements for the collection, use, and protection of personal data, including sensitive mental health information. Adhering to these regulations is paramount for building trust with patients and ensuring the responsible development and deployment of AI in mental healthcare. The GDPR, which applies to organizations operating in the European Union (EU) and the European Economic Area (EEA), grants individuals significant control over their personal data. It requires organizations to obtain explicit consent from individuals before collecting or using their data, to provide transparent information about how their data is being used, and to allow individuals to access, correct, or delete their data.

The CCPA, which applies to businesses operating in California, grants California residents similar rights over their personal data. It requires businesses to disclose what personal information they collect, how they use it, and with whom they share it. It also gives consumers the right to opt out of the sale of their personal information and to request that businesses delete their personal information. These protections are pivotal in reassuring individuals and safeguarding the sensitive information that AI accesses.

Organizations that use AI in mental healthcare must comply with the GDPR and the CCPA, as well as other applicable data privacy laws. This includes implementing appropriate data security measures, providing transparent privacy policies, and obtaining valid consent from individuals before collecting or using their data. Failure to comply with data privacy laws can result in significant fines and reputational damage, undermining trust in AI-driven solutions. Navigating the complexities of these laws requires careful planning and a commitment to protecting patient privacy.

The role of government agencies in regulating AI in mental health.

Government agencies play a crucial role in shaping the regulatory landscape for AI in mental health, ensuring that these technologies are developed and deployed in a safe, ethical, and responsible manner. These agencies are responsible for setting standards, enforcing regulations, and providing guidance to promote innovation while safeguarding patient rights and public well-being. In the United States, the Food and Drug Administration (FDA) regulates AI-powered tools that are used for diagnosis, treatment, or prevention of disease. The FDA requires that these tools be safe, effective, and properly labeled, and it may require manufacturers to conduct clinical trials to demonstrate the safety and effectiveness of their products.

The Federal Trade Commission (FTC) is responsible for protecting consumers from unfair or deceptive business practices. The FTC may investigate AI systems that make false or misleading claims, discriminate against certain groups of individuals, or violate consumer privacy laws. In Europe, the European Commission is responsible for setting the overall policy framework for AI. The Commission has proposed a new AI Act that would establish a risk-based approach to regulating AI, with stricter requirements for high-risk AI systems, such as those used in healthcare.

These agencies can provide guidance to businesses, provide rules to follow and also take action against companies or people who don't follow those rules. This power is an important part of ensuring AI protects people and is fair and objective. As AI becomes more widespread, these government organizations will help shape how it evolves and is managed. This will protect consumers and make it safer for people to get the support they need.

Building Trust and Acceptance: Addressing Concerns about AI

Addressing common concerns about using AI in mental healthcare: job displacement, dehumanization.

One of the most significant hurdles to the widespread adoption of AI in mental healthcare is building trust and acceptance among both professionals and the public. This requires directly addressing common concerns surrounding job displacement and the potential for dehumanization of care. Fear of job displacement is a very legitimate concern for many therapists and mental health professionals. They may worry that AI-powered tools will automate their tasks, reducing the need for human providers. While AI has the potential to automate some administrative tasks and provide certain types of support, it is unlikely to completely replace human therapists.

Instead, AI is more likely to augment their capabilities, freeing them up to focus on more complex and nuanced aspects of patient care. The potential for dehumanization is another valid concern. Some people fear that AI-powered tools will reduce the human connection and empathy that are essential for effective mental healthcare. It's important to recognize that AI is a tool, and it's up to humans to use it in a way that is consistent with ethical and compassionate care. AI should never be used to replace human interaction altogether.

These are both understandable concerns from people in the industry and outside of it, so it's important to take them into account. AI should serve as a support and enhancement. By addressing these fears, and being thoughtful and measured with the adoption, it can lead to better acceptance. As those working with AI show how it makes lives easier and more productive, it will make it much easier for adoption and trust.

Strategies for building trust and acceptance: transparency, education, and involving stakeholders in the development process.

Building trust and acceptance in AI-driven mental healthcare necessitates a multi-pronged approach that emphasizes transparency, education, and the active involvement of all stakeholders in the development process. These strategies aim to demystify AI, address legitimate concerns, and foster a sense of ownership and collaboration. Transparency is paramount for building trust in AI systems. This means being open about how AI algorithms work, what data they use, and how they make decisions. Explaining these processes to patients, professionals and others can help combat fears and misunderstanding.

Education is equally important. Many people have limited knowledge about AI and its potential applications in mental healthcare. Providing clear, accessible, and unbiased information about AI can help to dispel myths, address concerns, and promote informed decision-making. Involving stakeholders in the development process is another crucial step. This includes patients, therapists, researchers, policymakers, and community members. Including their voices helps in building consensus.

These strategies are important in showing the benefits of AI in mental health. By creating transparency, educating the public and working collaboratively, the trust will grow. As that happens, it will make AI an invaluable tool for improving millions of lives.

The importance of human oversight and ethical guidelines.

Even with advanced AI systems, human oversight and clear ethical guidelines remain paramount for ensuring responsible and beneficial implementation in mental healthcare. While AI can augment human capabilities and automate certain tasks, it should not replace the critical role of human judgment, empathy, and ethical decision-making. Human oversight is essential for monitoring AI systems, identifying potential biases or errors, and ensuring that they are used in a way that is consistent with ethical principles and professional standards. Clinicians should have the ability to review and override AI recommendations, taking into account the individual circumstances of each patient.

Ethical guidelines are needed to provide a framework for the responsible development and deployment of AI in mental healthcare. These guidelines should address issues such as data privacy, data security, algorithmic bias, transparency, and accountability. They should also emphasize the importance of human dignity, autonomy, and beneficence. These guidelines are important as they can be followed by the medical and AI community to ensure people are protected.

AI is a technology that can be extremely helpful, but it is not a replacement for human oversight. It will be up to humans to ensure AI is used in an ethical, equitable and trustworthy manner. This is also key to gaining more acceptance with the wider public, ensuring that the patients are getting the best care.

Infrastructure and Investment: Scaling AI Solutions
The need for adequate infrastructure to support the widespread adoption of AI in mental healthcare.

The widespread adoption of AI in mental healthcare hinges on the availability of adequate infrastructure, encompassing robust data systems, reliable technology, and skilled personnel. Without sufficient infrastructure, the potential benefits of AI may remain unrealized, particularly in underserved communities and resource-constrained settings. Robust data systems are essential for training and deploying AI models. This includes access to large, diverse, and well-curated datasets that accurately reflect the populations being served. These systems also need to ensure data privacy and security.

Reliable technology is needed to support the development and deployment of AI applications. This includes access to powerful computing resources, such as cloud computing platforms and specialized hardware, as well as the necessary software and tools for AI development. Skilled personnel are needed to develop, deploy, and maintain AI systems, as well as to interpret and apply the results in clinical practice. This includes data scientists, AI engineers, clinicians, and other healthcare professionals who are trained in the use of AI.

The widespread access and support of AI systems is key to ensuring equal access to this support for all people. When AI infrastructure is strong, it leads to better outcomes, and that requires effort and consideration. By focusing on building the infrastructure, it will also make it easier for AI tools to be adopted.

Investment in research and development, data infrastructure, and training programs.

Scaling AI solutions in mental healthcare necessitates strategic investments across various domains, including research and development, data infrastructure, and comprehensive training programs. These investments are crucial for driving innovation, ensuring data quality and accessibility, and equipping the workforce with the skills needed to effectively utilize AI technologies. Increased funding for research and development is essential for advancing the science of AI in mental healthcare. This includes supporting basic research to improve AI algorithms and techniques, as well as applied research to develop and test new AI-powered interventions.

Investment in data infrastructure is needed to create and maintain high-quality datasets that can be used to train and validate AI models. This includes funding for data collection, data curation, and data sharing initiatives. It also includes investing in data security and privacy measures to protect patient information. Well-funded data infrastructure can allow more people to access support. The data can also be used to further refine and improve AI systems.

Training programs are important in providing information and guidance to therapists and medical professionals to help them use AI effectively. With training and education, AI can be used in a safe and beneficial way. The costs of training and development are essential to making this technology a success. By having clear and comprehensive programs, it allows medical staff to feel more comfortable using and trusting the systems. Investment in these areas makes it easier to bring these systems to everyone.

Public-private partnerships for scaling AI solutions.

Scaling AI solutions in mental healthcare effectively requires strategic collaboration between public and private entities, leveraging their respective strengths and resources to accelerate innovation and ensure widespread adoption. These partnerships can foster a synergistic environment, combining the research expertise and public service mission of government agencies with the technological innovation and market reach of private companies. Public-private partnerships can fa-

67

cilitate the development and validation of AI-powered interventions through joint research initiatives.

Government agencies can provide access to data, expertise, and funding, while private companies can contribute their technological expertise and resources for developing and testing new AI applications. These partnerships also help drive the adoption of AI. By working together, public and private organizations can build trust and acceptance in AI, address ethical concerns, and ensure that AI is used in a responsible and equitable manner.

Public and private partnerships can also enable the development of scalable and sustainable AI solutions. Private companies can bring their expertise in product development, marketing, and distribution to help bring AI-powered interventions to a wider audience. This will help lead to the use of AI to make things better for millions of people. Public-private partnerships can be key to getting more AI support to more people in need.

The Human-AI Partnership: Collaboration and Synergy

The Role of Therapists in the Age of AI: Collaboration and Adaptation

How therapists can collaborate with AI to enhance their practice.

The integration of AI into mental healthcare is not about replacing therapists but about empowering them to enhance their practice and provide more effective care through strategic collaboration. By embracing AI as a valuable tool, therapists can augment their skills, improve their efficiency, and personalize treatment plans to better meet the needs of their patients. AI can assist therapists by providing them with real-time feedback during sessions, helping them to identify subtle cues in patient behavior and adjust their communication style accordingly. AI can also analyze patient data to identify patterns and trends that might otherwise be missed, providing therapists with valuable insights into their patients' mental health conditions.

AI can help with time consuming tasks, such as paperwork and scheduling,

69

which will free up more of the therapists time. This then allows them to focus on the actual practice of helping their patients. It's vital that therapists focus on how they can leverage the systems to improve. The human connection cannot be understated.

This collaborative approach not only enhances the therapist's capabilities but can lead to stronger relationships with their clients, better outcomes, and increased satisfaction. This is a new era of mental healthcare, and humans and AI must work together to make it better than ever. AI helps therapists become even better at their jobs.

Using AI to automate administrative tasks, gather data, and personalize treatment plans.

A significant advantage of integrating AI into therapeutic practices lies in its ability to automate administrative tasks, streamline data collection, and facilitate the creation of personalized treatment plans. This allows therapists to dedicate more time and energy to direct patient care, fostering stronger therapeutic relationships and improving overall outcomes. Automating administrative tasks frees up therapists from time-consuming paperwork, scheduling, and billing processes. AI-powered tools can handle these tasks efficiently and accurately, reducing the administrative burden on therapists and allowing them to focus on their core responsibilities.

AI can also streamline data collection by automatically gathering information from various sources, such as electronic health records, wearable sensors, and patient-reported outcomes. This data can be used to track patient progress, identify potential risks, and personalize treatment plans. Personalization is key to making sure that patients are getting care and support that suits them and their unique situation. There is no one-size-fits-all approach to mental healthcare.

By integrating AI in these areas, it makes the processes easier for both the therapist and the client. When time and resources are freed up, that means more time for meaningful connection and support for those in need. Automation makes therapists more effective. This is vital for the future of mental healthcare.

The importance of empathy, intuition, and human connection in therapy.

Despite the growing capabilities of AI, empathy, intuition, and human connection remain indispensable elements of effective therapy, forming the foundation of trust and facilitating deep, transformative healing. These uniquely human qualities cannot be replicated by machines and are essential for creating a safe and supportive therapeutic environment. Empathy, the ability to understand and share the feelings of another, is crucial for building rapport and trust with patients. Therapists use empathy to connect with their patients on a human level, validating their experiences and creating a sense of being understood.

Intuition, the ability to understand something instinctively, without the need for conscious reasoning, is another valuable asset for therapists. Therapists often rely on their intuition to pick up on subtle cues in patient behavior, identify underlying emotional patterns, and guide the therapeutic process. Human connection, the sense of belonging and connectedness that comes from meaningful social interactions, is essential for mental wellbeing. Therapy provides a space for individuals to connect with a caring and supportive therapist, fostering a sense of hope and resilience.

Those things are so important as the AI is there to support but not to replace a therapist. These key traits help ensure that clients are getting the best support possible. The human element is key to ensuring quality outcomes. The human touch will always be needed.

Training and Education: Preparing Mental Health Professionals for the Future

The need for training and education programs to prepare mental health professionals for the age of AI.

The successful integration of AI into mental healthcare hinges on equipping mental health professionals with the knowledge, skills, and ethical frameworks necessary to navigate this evolving landscape. Comprehensive training and education programs are essential for preparing therapists and other providers to effectively utilize AI tools, interpret their results, and maintain the highest standards of patient care. Traditional training programs for mental health professionals may not ade-

71

quately address the challenges and opportunities presented by AI.

There is a need for new curricula that specifically focus on AI literacy, data privacy, algorithmic bias, and ethical considerations. This will help those professionals understand how AI is being used, and where the potential issues lie. In addition to theoretical knowledge, training programs should also provide hands-on experience with AI-powered tools. This will help professionals develop the practical skills needed to use AI effectively in their practice.

This education is key to helping provide the best care possible for patients. These new systems should be taught so there is trust, ethical use, and support for the patients. In an ever-evolving field, education is paramount. This education will also allow for less resistance and more adoption.

Curriculum development: AI literacy, ethics, and practical applications.

Effective training and education for mental health professionals in the age of AI requires a carefully designed curriculum that encompasses AI literacy, ethical considerations, and practical applications. This holistic approach will empower professionals to understand the technology, use it responsibly, and integrate it seamlessly into their practice. AI literacy is essential for all mental health professionals, regardless of their specific role. This includes a basic understanding of AI concepts, algorithms, and applications, as well as the ability to critically evaluate AI-related claims and research findings.

Ethical considerations are paramount in the development of AI-related curriculum. Students should be taught about data privacy, algorithmic bias, transparency, and accountability, as well as the ethical implications of using AI in mental healthcare. Training should also cover the limitations of AI and the importance of maintaining human oversight. Curricula should also focus on the practical applications of AI in mental healthcare, providing students with hands-on experience using AI-powered tools for diagnosis, treatment planning, and therapy.

Students should learn how to integrate AI into their practice in a way that enhances their skills and improves patient outcomes. The practical applications are an important element, as it can help to build trust in the systems and provide value for their use. Through this course of study, professionals can feel confident in their knowledge of how to use AI to improve their practices. As AI evolves, the curriculum must adapt to continue to ensure safety and effective implementation.

Opportunities for continuing education and professional development.

Given the rapid pace of innovation in AI, mental health professionals must have access to ongoing opportunities for continuing education and professional development to stay abreast of the latest advancements and best practices. These opportunities should be accessible, affordable, and tailored to the specific needs of different professional roles. Continuing education programs can provide mental health professionals with in-depth knowledge and skills in specific areas of AI, such as machine learning, natural language processing, or virtual reality therapy.

These programs can be offered through universities, professional organizations, or online learning platforms. Professional development workshops and conferences can provide mental health professionals with opportunities to network with experts, share best practices, and learn about emerging trends in AI. These events can also offer hands-on training and demonstrations of AI-powered tools. As AI becomes more integrated, it is important for mental health professionals to stay current on all of the available tools and applications.

By ensuring access to high-quality continuing education and professional development opportunities, the field can empower mental health professionals to effectively use AI to improve patient outcomes. This continued learning and education will make AI tools more widespread and trustworthy. That can only lead to better support for those who need it. The investment is key to the process.

The Future of Mental Healthcare: A Vision of Collaboration and Innovation

Envisioning a future where AI and human professionals work together to provide personalized, accessible, and effective mental healthcare.

The future of mental healthcare is not one dominated by machines, but rather a harmonious partnership between AI and human professionals, working in synergy to deliver personalized, accessible, and effective care. This collaborative vision leverages the strengths of both AI and human expertise, creating a system that is more efficient, equitable, and compassionate. Imagine a world where AI-powered tools are seamlessly integrated into every aspect of mental healthcare, from early detection and diagnosis to treatment planning and ongoing support.

AI algorithms analyze vast amounts of data to identify individuals at risk, personalize treatment plans based on individual needs, and provide real-time feedback to therapists during sessions. Therapists then use this information to deliver more targeted and effective interventions, building stronger relationships with their patients and fostering a sense of trust and hope. This approach gives clients and professionals more opportunities to help each other to get better. As the technology grows and improves, so will the methods of care.

AI eliminates barriers to access and providing support whenever and wherever it's needed. AI empowers professionals, rather than replacing them. This is a new era of care that will be available to everyone.

The potential for AI to transform the field of mental health and improve the lives of millions of people.

The potential for AI to revolutionize mental health and improve the lives of millions is truly vast, offering hope for a future where mental wellbeing is prioritized, accessible, and effectively addressed for all. By harnessing the power of AI, the field can overcome many of the long-standing challenges that have hindered progress, creating a more equitable and compassionate system of care. The AI's capabilities can greatly improve mental health, such as helping with the workload that therapists face.

This support will not only improve the lives of the patients who are getting care, but also will improve the lives of the people providing care. By focusing on AI and human collaboration, it will allow the work to get done more effectively. It also allows AI to eliminate

74

some of the challenges of access, such as location or cost, and support people wherever and whenever they need it.

The transformations made with the help of AI can not only improve people's lives, but truly save them as well. Access to quicker support and better care leads to better overall outcomes for people who are struggling. This transformation, powered by AI, can drastically change the scope of mental healthcare for years to come.

Future Trends and Innovations: What Lies Ahead?

The Metaverse and Mental Health: Virtual Reality Therapy and Social Support

Exploring the potential of the metaverse for mental health: virtual reality therapy, social support groups, and gamified interventions.

The metaverse, a persistent, shared virtual world, presents exciting new frontiers for mental healthcare, offering immersive experiences that can enhance therapy, foster social support, and promote engagement through gamified interventions. While still in its early stages, the metaverse holds immense potential for transforming how mental health services are delivered and accessed. Virtual reality therapy, for example, can be significantly enhanced within the metaverse. Individuals can confront their fears, practice social skills, or process traumatic experiences in a safe and controlled virtual environment.

AI-powered avatars can act as virtual therapists or support group facilitators, providing personalized guidance and encouragement. The metaverse can provide opportuni-

77

ties for those who may not be able to access care. The digital divide may also be reduced, as the barrier to entry may be lessened through new programs and initiatives. These types of support groups can also allow access to more options.

The Metaverse presents unique opportunities, and these are just some of the things that can be done. The immersive nature of this technology can open doors that were never open before, and it's something the medical field can continue to explore to help get support to people. These new virtual options can make all the difference in many lives.

Benefits of virtual reality therapy: immersive experiences, reduced stigma, and increased access to care.

Virtual reality (VR) therapy, particularly within the metaverse, offers a compelling range of benefits for mental healthcare, including immersive experiences, reduced stigma, and increased access to care. These advantages can significantly enhance treatment outcomes and improve the overall well-being of individuals. The immersive nature of VR therapy allows individuals to fully engage with the therapeutic environment, creating a more realistic and emotionally engaging experience. This can be particularly helpful for treating anxiety disorders, phobias, and PTSD, where exposure to triggering stimuli is a key component of treatment.

Individuals may feel safer and more comfortable confronting their fears in a virtual setting compared to real-world situations. VR therapy can also help to reduce stigma associated with seeking mental health care. Some individuals may feel embarrassed or ashamed about seeking traditional therapy, but they may be more willing to engage with VR therapy in the privacy of their own homes. The reduction of stigma is crucial for making treatment more accessible. This can help to promote mental health, which then reduces problems in their life.

As access to care increases, there is a greater ability to get people the treatment they need. VR has no limits to location, therefore, anyone can access it from anywhere in the world. VR also reduces issues around cost, as the treatment plans will be much more affordable. This is key to making mental healthcare more accessible to people.

Challenges and ethical considerations: digital divide, safety, and privacy.
While the metaverse holds exciting potential for mental healthcare, it's crucial to acknowledge and address the inherent challenges and ethical considerations, including the digital divide, safety concerns, and data privacy. These issues must be carefully navigated to ensure equitable access and responsible implementation. The digital divide, the gap between those who have access to technology and those who do not, is a significant concern. Access to VR headsets, high-speed internet, and the metaverse itself may be limited by socioeconomic factors, creating disparities in access to VR therapy and social support.

Efforts must be made to bridge this divide, ensuring that VR therapy is accessible to individuals from all backgrounds. Safety is another important consideration. The immersive nature of VR can be disorienting or triggering for some individuals, and it's essential to provide appropriate support and guidance to prevent adverse effects. There is also a need to address potential risks related to cyberbullying, harassment, and exposure to inappropriate content within the metaverse.

Data privacy is a paramount concern. The metaverse relies on the collection and analysis of vast amounts of personal data, raising concerns about how this data is being used, stored, and protected. It is crucial to implement robust data privacy measures to safeguard individuals' personal information and prevent unauthorized access. The future holds incredible potential, but these things need to be taken into consideration. By being thoughtful and considerate, the future can be bright for the technology and for the healthcare system.

AI-Powered Wearables: Monitoring Mental Health in Real-Time
Using AI-powered wearables to monitor mental health in real-time: heart rate, sleep patterns, and activity levels.

AI-powered wearable devices are poised to revolutionize mental health monitoring by providing continuous, real-time data on key physiological indicators, offering valuable insights into an individual's emotional and cognitive state. These devices, equipped with advanced sensors and AI algorithms, can track heart rate, sleep patterns, activity levels, and other metrics, providing a comprehensive picture of an individual's mental wellbeing. Heart rate variability (HRV), the variation in time intervals between heartbeats, is a sensitive indicator of stress, anxiety, and emotional regulation.

AI algorithms can analyze HRV data to detect changes in an individual's stress levels, identify patterns of anxiety, and assess their overall emotional state. Sleep patterns are closely linked to mental health, with sleep disturbances often being a symptom of depression, anxiety, and other conditions. AI-powered wearables can track sleep duration, sleep quality, and sleep stages, providing insights into an individual's sleep patterns and identifying potential sleep-related problems. Changes in activity can show how the person is doing as well.

By continuously monitoring these physiological indicators, AI-powered wearables can provide a valuable tool for early detection, personalized treatment, and ongoing support. These are just a few examples of how this technology can change the way we are able to provide support. As more data can be analyzed, there is an increased opportunity to understand how to best care for an individual. The insights are a benefit for professionals and clients.

Analyzing data to identify patterns and predict mental health crises.

The true power of AI-powered wearables lies in their ability to analyze the collected data, identify subtle patterns, and predict potential mental health crises before they escalate. By recognizing these warning signs, timely interventions can be implemented, potentially preventing significant harm and improving outcomes. AI algorithms can be trained to identify patterns in physiological data that are associated with an increased risk of depression, anxiety, or suicidal ideation.

For example, a sudden increase in heart rate, a disruption in sleep patterns, or a decrease in physical activity could be warning signs of an impending mental health crisis. By monitoring these patterns over time, AI can provide early alerts to healthcare providers, allowing them to intervene before the individual experiences a full-blown crisis. These early interventions can have a significant impact on the individuals care.

Having clear action plans is essential for addressing these things.

These things are the tools that doctors have long needed and with AI it can become a reality. Having the tools in place for early intervention can not only improve but also save lives. While it's never perfect, the information is there to help support those in need. These are some truly special capabilities to leverage.

The Role of AI in Prevention: Promoting Mental Wellbeing and Resilience

Using AI to promote mental wellbeing and resilience: personalized stress management programs, mindfulness exercises, and social support networks.

The future of mental healthcare extends beyond treatment to proactive prevention, with AI playing a crucial role in promoting mental wellbeing and building resilience. By leveraging personalized stress management programs, facilitating access to mindfulness exercises, and strengthening social support networks, AI can empower individuals to take control of their mental health and thrive. Personalized stress management programs tailored to individual needs and preferences are important for ensuring that clients have the support they need. AI can analyze individual data, identify patterns, and help clients.

AI can also be used to facilitate access to mindfulness exercises by providing personalized guidance, tracking progress, and offering support. This can allow clients to work through issues on their own. This allows the client to have the power and control over their own plan. These programs not only target stress, but also encourage individuals to be more proactive about their mental health.

AI offers support that removes roadblocks for people to manage their well being. With access to these systems and programs, clients can find a path to building up their resilience. Providing support and removing roadblocks is key to allowing clients to get better faster.

Targeting at-risk populations and addressing social determinants of mental health.

To maximize the impact of AI in promoting mental wellbeing and resilience, targeted efforts are essential to address the needs of at-risk populations and mitigate the adverse effects of social determinants of health. AI can help identify these populations and deliver tailored interventions to those who need it most. Certain populations are at higher risk for mental health conditions due to factors such as poverty, discrimination, trauma, or social isolation. AI can be used to analyze data from various sources to identify these at-risk populations and understand their specific needs.

This can allow healthcare providers and community organizations to develop targeted prevention programs that address the root causes of mental health problems. These programs should focus on promoting protective factors, such as social support, coping skills, and access to resources. The effectiveness of these programs can be tracked and analyzed through AI systems to allow organizations to make improvements and increase outcomes. By reaching these groups, it provides help to those who need it most.

Using AI to look at the social factors that lead to health can provide new avenues for approaching support and prevention. These focused methods allow all people to have support no matter their situation. Reaching everyone is the key goal for the future.

The importance of early intervention and prevention efforts.

The future of mental healthcare must prioritize early intervention and prevention efforts, recognizing that addressing mental health challenges before they escalate is far more effective and humane than simply treating them after they become severe. AI offers powerful tools for identifying individuals at risk, delivering targeted interventions, and promoting mental wellbeing from the earliest stages of life. The old saying that an ounce of prevention is worth a pound of cure certainly applies to mental health.

Early intervention and prevention efforts can reduce the likelihood of developing chronic mental health conditions, improve overall quality of life, and reduce the burden on healthcare systems. AI is not a simple or immediate fix, but it can provide a more efficient, accessible, and effective pathway for the future. It has the ability to look at a wide range of data and make determinations that humans may not see. When used in a thoughtful way, that can have a real impact.

These tools are also powerful for helping provide the best care for those who may be struggling. In general, it can lead to happier and healthier lives for people around the world. The future is very promising in this world.

Embracing the Future with Optimism and Caution

Recap of Key Insights: The Transformative Potential of AI in Mental Health

Summarizing the key insights from the book: the potential of AI to address gaps in mental healthcare access, affordability, and quality.

As we reach the conclusion of this exploration into the intersection of AI and mental health, it is crucial to revisit the key insights that have emerged, highlighting the transformative potential of AI in addressing long-standing gaps in access, affordability, and quality of care. Throughout this book, it has been shown the way that AI is a powerful and positive force for good. However, it's equally important to proceed with caution and consideration to protect individuals.

AI-powered solutions offer the ability to revolutionize mental healthcare. These include tools for automated support and care to AI-assisted analysis and planning. This alone will greatly increase the number of people who are able to access care, regardless of their location or socio-economic standing. All of these

85

things can be leveraged to make things better for people all over the world.

There are many reasons to be excited and to also use caution as we begin to implement these new programs. By summarizing these ideas, people can take them forward and use the information to drive positive change in this realm. The future has real potential to be very bright for mental healthcare.

Highlighting the ethical considerations and challenges that need to be addressed.

While the potential of AI to transform mental healthcare is undeniable, it is equally essential to acknowledge and address the ethical considerations and challenges that accompany its integration. Navigating these complexities is crucial for ensuring that AI is used responsibly, ethically, and in a way that benefits all members of society. The ethical concerns need to be carefully and thoughtfully considered so people are protected. These things include maintaining data privacy, preventing algorithms from being used for harmful activity, and ensuring appropriate oversight.

There are many groups and communities who have historically struggled with being able to have trust in the medical community. It's important to acknowledge that and work to improve the systems so they are truly helpful to everyone. These systems and the implementation can play a part in promoting or preventing ethical harm. These issues need to be brought into the light so they are openly discussed.

By thoughtfully approaching these topics, it will allow the AI systems to be implemented and improve the lives of everyone. By being proactive, ethical concerns can be managed from the outset. This can lead to the overall improvement of access, awareness and positive outcomes for all patients.

Emphasizing the importance of human oversight and collaboration.

As this book nears completion, one message needs to be made clear: while AI holds immense promise for revolutionizing mental healthcare, it is crucial to emphasize the ongoing importance of human oversight and collaboration. AI should not be viewed as a replacement for human professionals, but rather as a tool to augment their skills and enhance their ability to provide compassionate and effective care. The human connection is not something that a computer can replicate.

While the tools can be helpful, it is crucial to have the human element. This makes patients feel safer and supported in their journey. AI systems need to be used to support, not replace, human interaction. This will also make sure that the systems are used ethically.

Human compassion, understanding, and insight are critical for this work, and it is important to ensure this is not lost. With both elements combined, better and more complete work can be done. The future should see more professionals trained and ready to use both human skills and AI tools to improve care.

Call to Action: Embracing the Future with Responsibility and Innovation
Encouraging readers to embrace the future of AI in mental health with optimism and caution.

As we stand on the cusp of a new era in mental healthcare, fueled by the power of artificial intelligence, it is imperative that we embrace this future with both optimism and caution. The opportunities for improving access, affordability, and quality of care are immense, but it is equally important to proceed thoughtfully and responsibly, ensuring that AI is used in a way that benefits all members of society. The potential for good is undeniable, and readers should feel excited about the possibilities for the future.

However, with progress also comes some level of risk. New problems and concerns may arise, and it is important to recognize that. There are so many possibilities, and it is a call to action to make sure that it moves forward. The chance to improve lives is there and should be approached with optimism.

By moving forward with this and using careful methods, it allows all the people to get quality healthcare in the best way. With this method, the future will be something to look forward to. This careful balance of enthusiasm and reflection is key to success.

Calling for responsible innovation, ethical development, and collaboration among stakeholders.

To realize the transformative potential of AI in mental health, it is imperative that we prioritize responsible innovation, ethical development, and robust collaboration among all stakeholders. These guiding principles will ensure that AI is used in a way that is consistent with human values, protects patient rights, and promotes equitable access to care. It is important to consider the risks as well as benefits of introducing AI into mental healthcare. It also should be developed in an ethical way.

There also needs to be open communication and collaboration in developing these new solutions. All voices should be heard so these tools make a difference for people. These innovative tools should be designed with ethics in mind. All of these things are needed to protect people.

It's important to engage with medical, technology, government and social fields. With all of those minds working together, it means there is greater potential for improved healthcare. It also means the systems are ethical, well-designed, and make improvements to the current system.

Empowering readers to become advocates for the responsible use of AI in mental healthcare.

The power to shape the future of AI in mental healthcare lies not just in the hands of researchers and developers, but in the collective action of informed and engaged individuals. It is our responsibility to become advocates for the responsible use of AI, ensuring that these technologies are used to promote mental wellbeing, reduce suffering, and advance social justice. Each reader should act as an advocate.

It is imperative to ask questions, ask for transparency, and support systems that have ethical approaches. With action and support, it can improve the industry and also improve the lives of the people who need the support. It is also up to those reading to learn more, and keep up with the times as AI continues to evolve.

By staying informed and helping to share information, more and more lives can be improved. Support the right approaches, hold companies and organizations responsible and be a voice for good. It takes everyone working together to make a difference.

The Journey Ahead: A Vision of Hope and Progress
A final message of hope and optimism about the future of mental healthcare.

As this journey through the landscape of AI and mental health concludes, let us carry forward a message of hope and unwavering optimism about the future. The potential for AI to transform the field, alleviate suffering, and promote mental wellbeing for all is immense, offering a vision of a brighter and more compassionate tomorrow. It is not all doom and gloom and AI will create a dystopian reality.

There is real hope and potential for millions of lives to be improved. With all of the support and new technology, it can truly be life changing for those who have not had support before. As AI evolves, it will continue to change, but by working together, we can harness AI for good.

It's important to be excited about new potential. While there will be challenges, it's important to remember that the future is not written in stone. AI can be a force for good to all.

Envisioning a world where AI helps to improve the lives of millions of people and promotes mental wellbeing for all.

Imagine a future where AI is seamlessly integrated into society, working quietly and efficiently behind the scenes to improve the lives of millions, promoting mental wellbeing for all, regardless of their background, location, or circumstances. This vision is not a utopian fantasy but a realistic possibility within our reach. This is a vision of hope and a world that is truly possible.

It will take hard work and commitment to see this vision come to fruition. New AI systems can reduce problems and provide support to those who need it, and it should be made available to the most people possible. Everyone deserves the right to great healthcare.

That support should be there, no matter who they are or where they are located. A world with the help of AI to get everyone the support they need is a beautiful idea that is also possible. With careful planning, commitment, and human oversight, AI can be a tool for positive change for everyone.

Encouraging readers to continue learning and exploring the potential of AI in mental health.

The journey into the world of AI and mental health does not end here. As you close this book, I encourage each of you to continue learning, exploring, and engaging with the transformative potential of AI in this vital field. The landscape of AI is constantly evolving, with new breakthroughs and applications emerging at an ever-accelerating pace. Staying informed about these developments is crucial for understanding the full scope of AI's potential impact on mental healthcare.

This exploration has just scratched the surface of what is possible in the years to come. It's up to everyone to continue the journey of understanding AI. By engaging with others and sharing ideas, it makes a significant difference to helping to share and expand those ideas.

There are countless resources, such as books, articles, and websites, to help people learn more. With the potential for AI to change mental healthcare for the better, it is worth taking the time to continue learning and exploring to make a difference in the lives of many people. The future is bright and it is time to embrace it.

Conclusion: Empowering You for the Future

The journey through the landscape of Artificial Intelligence and its potential to re-shape mental healthcare has, hopefully, illuminated both the extraordinary opportunities and the critical responsibilities that lie ahead. As we stand at this pivotal juncture, it is no longer sufficient to simply observe the unfolding of these technologies; rather, it is imperative that each of us actively participate in shaping their trajectory, ensuring that AI serves as a force for good, promoting mental wellbeing, and fostering a more equitable and compassionate society. This concluding section is designed to empower you, the reader, with the knowledge, perspective, and actionable insights needed to become an informed advocate, a responsible innovator, and a catalyst for positive change within the realm of AI and mental health.

The preceding chapters have painted a detailed picture of the current mental health crisis, characterized by limited access, soaring costs, persistent stigma, and the exacerbating effects of global events. We have explored the limitations of traditional approaches and the promise of AI to bridge these gaps, offering personalized support, early detection, and enhanced therapeutic interventions. We have delved into the inner workings of generative AI, demystifying complex concepts and showcasing its potential for creating engaging educational content, tailored mindfulness programs, and novel avenues for creative expression.

Yet, alongside this optimism, we have also confronted the ethical minefield that accompanies the deployment of AI in sensitive domains like mental healthcare. Issues of data privacy, algorithmic bias, transparency, and accountability have been brought to the forefront, underscoring the need for careful consideration, proactive mitigation strategies, and robust ethical frameworks. It is in this delicate balance between embracing innovation and exercising caution that the true power of AI can be unlocked, paving the way for a future where mental wellbeing is accessible to all.

The Path Forward: A Synthesis of Key Principles

Before charting a course for the future, it is essential to synthesize the key principles that have emerged throughout this exploration. These principles serve as guiding lights, illuminating the path towards responsible innovation and ethical implementation:

- Human-Centered Design: At the heart of every AI solution must lie a deep understanding of human needs, values, and experiences. AI should be designed to augment, not replace, human connection, empathy, and intuition, prioritizing patient autonomy and well-being above all else.
- Data Responsibility: Data privacy and security must be paramount. Stringent measures must be implemented to protect sensitive patient information, ensuring that data is collected, used, and stored in compliance with ethical and legal guidelines. Algorithmic bias must be actively identified and mitigated, striving for fairness and equity in all AI-driven decisions.
- Transparency and Explainability: AI systems should be as transparent and explainable as possible, allowing users to understand how decisions are made and what factors are taken into consideration. Black box algorithms should be avoided in favor of models that can be readily interpreted and understood by both clinicians and

patients.
- Collaboration and Inclusivity: The development and deployment of AI in mental healthcare should be a collaborative and inclusive process, involving all stakeholders, including patients, therapists, researchers, policymakers, and community members. Diverse perspectives should be actively sought and incorporated to ensure that AI solutions are culturally sensitive, equitable, and responsive to the needs of all populations.
- Continuous Monitoring and Evaluation: AI systems should be continuously monitored and evaluated to assess their performance, identify potential biases or errors, and ensure that they are meeting their intended goals. Feedback mechanisms should be implemented to allow users to report concerns and contribute to ongoing improvements.

Actionable Steps: Empowering You to Make a Difference

Now, let us translate these guiding principles into actionable steps that you, as a reader and a member of society, can take to contribute to the responsible development and deployment of AI in mental healthcare:
- Become an Informed Advocate: The first and most important step is to educate yourself about AI and its potential impact on mental health. Read books, articles, and research papers, attend conferences and workshops, and engage in discussions with experts in the field. The more you know, the better equipped you will be to advocate for responsible innovation and ethical practices. Critically evaluate the claims made by AI developers and healthcare providers, seeking evidence-based information and questioning any claims that seem too good to be true.
- Support Research and Innovation: Advocate for increased funding for research and development in AI for mental health, both from government agencies and private organizations. Support initiatives that focus on developing and testing new AI-powered interventions, as well as research that addresses ethical considerations and promotes responsible innovation. Encourage interdisciplinary collaboration between AI researchers, mental health professionals, and other stakeholders.
- Promote Data Privacy and Security: Advocate for strong data pri-

vacy laws and regulations that protect patient health information. Support organizations that are working to develop and implement secure data sharing practices that enable AI research while safeguarding patient privacy. Be mindful of your own data privacy practices, taking steps to protect your personal information online and being cautious about sharing sensitive data with AI systems.

- Demand Transparency and Explainability: Encourage AI developers and healthcare providers to prioritize transparency and explainability in their systems. Support initiatives that are working to develop XAI techniques and promote the use of interpretable AI models. Ask questions about how AI systems work, what data they use, and how they make decisions.

- Champion Equity and Fairness: Advocate for the development and deployment of AI systems that are fair, equitable, and accessible to all members of society, regardless of their background, race, ethnicity, socioeconomic status, or other factors. Support initiatives that are working to mitigate algorithmic bias and promote data diversity. Demand accountability from AI developers and healthcare providers for ensuring that their systems do not perpetuate existing inequalities.

- Engage in Ethical Discussions: Participate in public discussions about the ethical implications of AI in mental healthcare. Share your thoughts, concerns, and perspectives with others, and listen to the viewpoints of those with different experiences. Advocate for the development of ethical guidelines and standards for the use of AI in mental health.

- Support Human-Centered Care: Remind everyone that AI should never replace human connection, empathy, and intuition. Champion the role of therapists and mental health professionals, and recognize their importance in providing compassionate and effective care. Advocate for training and education programs that equip mental health professionals with the skills needed to effectively collaborate with AI.

- Hold Companies Accountable: As consumers and potential users of AI-driven mental health tools, exercise your power to hold companies accountable for responsible development and deployment. Research the privacy policies, data security measures, and ethical guidelines of AI providers before using their products or services. Voice your concerns to companies that are not transparent or ethical in their practices.

- Engage with Policymakers: Contact your elected officials and advocate for policies that support responsible innovation in AI for mental health. Encourage them to invest in research and development, promote data privacy and security, and address ethical considerations. Support legislation that promotes equitable access to mental healthcare, regardless of socioeconomic status or geographic location.
- Spread Awareness: Share your knowledge and insights about AI in mental health with others. Talk to your friends, family members, and colleagues about the potential benefits and risks of these technologies. Use social media, blogs, and other platforms to raise awareness and promote informed discussions.

The Future is Now: Embracing the Challenge and Seizing the Opportunity

The future of mental healthcare is not a distant dream; it is a reality that is unfolding before our eyes. AI has the power to transform the field in profound ways, but it is up to us to ensure that this transformation is guided by wisdom, compassion, and a commitment to ethical principles. By embracing the challenge and seizing the opportunity, we can create a future where mental wellbeing is prioritized, accessible, and effectively supported for all.

This is not a task for a select few, but a collective endeavor that requires the participation of all members of society. Whether you are a mental health professional, an AI researcher, a policymaker, a patient, or simply a concerned citizen, your voice matters and your actions can make a difference. The journey ahead will not be without its challenges, but the potential rewards are too great to ignore.

Let us embark on this path with optimism, courage, and a shared vision of a future where mental health is valued, supported, and accessible to all. It is time to empower ourselves, embrace innovation, and build a world where everyone has the opportunity to thrive. This is about so much more than improving practices. This is about creating long-lasting and meaningful transformation across the world for millions of people.

This is what is at stake if AI is not implemented with these goals in mind. Now is the time to act! This will lead to true and lasting results.

We hope that you enjoyed this book.
We would really appreciate if you could take
a couple of minutes to leave us a review on Amazon.
Thank you again from all of us at Purple Fox Publications.

www.ingramcontent.com/pod-product-compliance
Lightning Source LLC
LaVergne TN
LVHW051746050326
832903LV00029B/2749